the
air
down
here

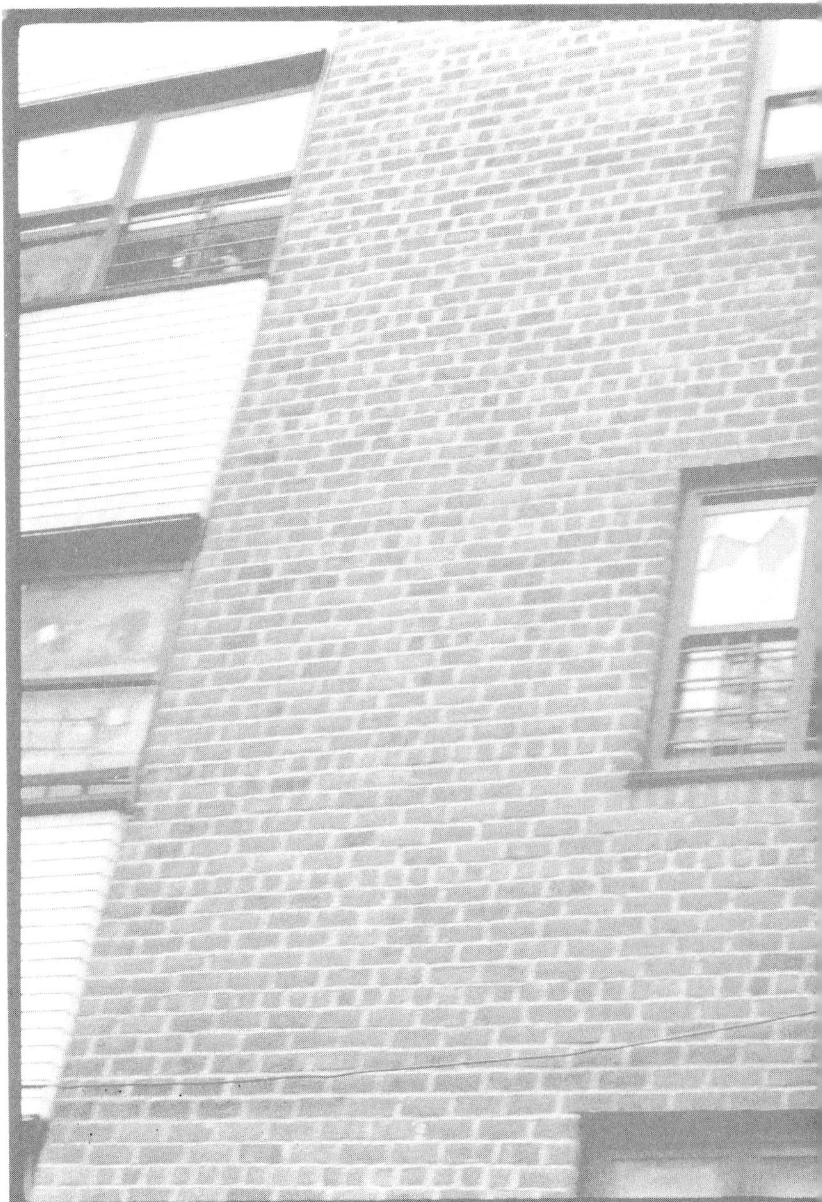

True Tales from a
South Bronx Boyhood

the
air
down
here

Gil C. Alicea
with Carmine DeSena

Photographs
by Gil C. Alicea

CHRONICLE BOOKS
SAN FRANCISCO

Printed in the United States of America.
Book and cover design by Laura Lovett
Cover photograph © 1995 by Michael Weisbrot

Library of Congress Cataloging-in-Publication Data

    Alicea, Gil C.
       The air down here: true tales from a South Bronx boyhood / Gil
    C. Alicea, with Carmine DeSena
       p.   cm.
    ISBN 0-8118-1048-8

    1. Hispanic american youth—New York (N.Y.)—Social conditions. 2.
    Bronx (New York, N.Y.)—Social conditions. 3. New York (N.Y.)—Social
    conditions. 4. Alicea, Gil C. I. DeSena, Carmine. II. Title.
    F128.9.S75A45   1995
    974.7'275043'092–dc20
    [B]   95-12962
                                CIP

Distributed in Canada by Raincoast Books
8680 Cambie Street, Vancouver, B.C. V6P 6M9

10 9 8 7 6 5 4 3 2 1

Chronicle Books
275 Fifth Street
San Francisco, CA 94103

This book is dedicated
to my Dad and the memory
of my mother, Maria, my
sister, Alexis, and my
grandmother, Isabelle. I
know you're watching over
me and I love you with
all my heart.   Gil

. . . .

I dedicate this book
to the memory of Bill,
who showed me life was like
an empty room: full of
options.   Carmine

Contents

Acknowledgments

Gil and Carmine would like to offer special thanks to
Barbara-J. Zitwer, Thom Leidner, and Karen Silver
for their support and guidance.

Gil offers thanks to his loving
family and friends: Aunt Carmen, Aunt Luz, Papo, Rosa,
Uncle Ruben, Aunt Elizabeth, cousin Richie, Uncle Danny, Aunt
Betty, Uncle Artie, cousin John, cousin Juan, cousin Dakota,
Danielle, Cindy, cousin Lisa, cousin Andy, cousin Jose, cousin
Steve, cousin Willy and all my friends.

A very special thanks to Denis Hamill.

Gil would also like to thank those wonderful people who are
helping make his dream come true: One Potata Productions—
Diane Mancher and Melinda Mullin; Annie and Dave Hausman;
Michael Regan; John Patterson, Jr.; South Bronx Overall
Economic Development Corp; and The Licitra Scholarship Fund.

Introduction

by Carmine
DeSena

As a writer, I have watched numerous projects emerge
from my pen and imagination. With this project, however,
in addition to a book, I witnessed the emergence of a boy
into young adulthood. From my first meeting with fifteen-
year-old Gil, I felt I already knew him, yet he would later
prove to be a constant puzzle. He knew more about the
designer clothing I was wearing than I did. He questioned
me about why and how I would work with him, and he
assessed me. I expected this to some degree, as I was
doing the same. But his questions were not of a business
nature. He was just curious. He wanted different experiences, and to a large extent I was one.

I had worried how I would relate to a teenager,

whose experience as a Hispanic American growing up in the housing projects of the South Bronx seemed so foreign to me. Strangely there was no awkwardness between us. Soon after our meeting began, I was struck, not by our differences, but by our similarities. I, too, had grown up in a money-tight situation and, like Gil, had nursed my mother through a devastating illness while still in my teens. Even these reasons, however, didn't fully explain why we were so in sync.

As the two of us wandered through the streets of Manhattan on that first day, I saw Gil reaching with his eyes. Grabbing with his eyes. Digesting with his eyes. He wanted to know things: not to have them, but to use them. He absorbed information so quickly that he could soon offer wry observations with the best social critics. I found this hunger of Gil's to echo my own. I remembered coming to Manhattan at age twelve with a friend and his parents and filling my own eyes the same way. It had aided me in deciding that I would spend my adult life on this island to absorb its culture.

So it was that we began our relationship. While we walked, our senses of humor and natural gifts of gab bonded us. I was impressed with his sharpness and optimism, characteristics which had served me well during my own troubled adolescence. Although Gil was in some ways more man than boy, his lunch request of pizza and chicken wings reminded me that he was still a kid, only fifteen. It was a relief of sorts.

Gil is best at communicating verbally. He is far more inhibited when he has to commit to the written word. To best foster his articulate storytelling in the oral tradition, this book was compiled via tape-recorded interviews. I then transcribed his words verbatim to maintain the accuracy of his voice. Gil then edited the pieces with me until he felt they accurately reflected his experiences.

I had no concerns about working together with Gil after our first meeting. There would always be a flow of conversation, and we would enjoy each other. To his credit, as his home situation grew increasingly more difficult, he became more dedicated to completing the project. I offered emotional support but felt weak in my inability to do anything more significant. I knew that whatever I could possibly do, it could not alter the harsh reality of his mother's slow death.

Gil managed his problems with perseverance—performing difficult tasks to ease his mother's suffering, while working out his aggression and fear playing basketball. At our meetings, no matter what problems had haunted him the night before, he was ready to work. When we finished, we would steal a few hours to play. We went to museums, shows, and stores, his eye always ready to feast. He seemed to be good at so many things, to have so much untapped talent at his disposal. However, whenever I began to think that he seemed more professor than student, he would pull a prank so completely outrageous and childish that I would be both furious and

and laughing hysterically. (His crowning achievement was handcuffing me to my pants in an elevator and telling an elderly couple that I had tried to abduct him.)

Gil countered our "buddy" relationship by also seeking my adult advice about the things that worried or interested him. I had not expected to feel like a friend, and certainly not a father, but I experienced both of these sensations and welcomed them. He gave me a perspective that I had needed desperately, without realizing it. I had so much in my life—family, success and confidence in my future—all of which had taken me decades to achieve. Yet I overlooked the joy these things offered. It was as if my happiness had become commonplace. I needed to explore again, even though I had already discovered. Gil gave me this perspective not with intent, but just as part of his being.

I became as interested in his love of sports as he did in my love of the arts. He worked on the heart-wrenching aspects of this book studiously and asked that I share my life with him as well. We fought to establish an objectivity in our work through an amazing closeness. We examined his successes and mistakes with the same energy. To this end, I think this book has truth. But it was only after finishing it, and putting it aside, that I fully understood what had transpired.

What I realized was that Gil, during the book project, was emerging from a crisis and growing into adulthood at the same time. These internal struggles made him question his beliefs, goals, and needs; the urban environment he lived in; and American society in general. More importantly, he began looking for his place: who he would be, what he would do, and what his future would be. This searching challenged him to reject the things most available and familiar to him. It asked that he expand beyond his neighborhood, family, and friends.

As the book continued to develop, I witnessed the contradiction of what he did versus his newly forming ideas, and I saw his need to rationalize and categorize his experiences to make better choices for the life he hoped for. He was becoming a man. As during every real growth process, there were numerous inconsistencies in Gil's thoughts and actions. His inability to come to terms with certain parts of his life, especially his past character and deeds, did not always result in successful transitions. There was always some falling back, some acting out of old behaviors. This caused him pain and disillusionment, but the sting—and ramifications—of repeating a mistake served to reinforce his new thoughts as being more positive and productive.

As you read this book, understand that you are reading about a year of struggle that will eventually lead young Gil, as his journey continues, to either a life of options or one of despair. Can he reject those parts of himself and his world that propel him to skip school, use drugs, and run with gangs? Or will his lust for knowledge and new experiences direct him to more mentally stimulating outlets, such as college? These are difficult questions, because the potential for both exists. In his favor, he is exceptionally bright and creative. He possesses the tools to succeed at what he wants, but there is always danger. This notion saddens me.

For all our country's interest in the world—other nations' wars, starving people, and devastation—it often overlooks the same problems right at home. There is a war on U.S. children. Its weapons are poverty, substandard education and housing, poor nutrition, and lack of hope. The outcomes are anger, crime, and drugs. These problems then perpetuate themselves. With each generation of children that grow up in this manner, we lose another battle . . . another million souls. These children need enrichment and exposure to new ideas. They have to be able to identify new options beyond the overwhelming ruins they experience. They have to see other worlds and know they exist. Only then can they aspire to make the changes they have to, to commit to achieving a more satisfying, fulfilling, and stabilized life.

I have witnessed this with Gil. Each new opportunity opened him up a little more. He is striving to broaden his horizons and grow into the adult he wants to be. It would not be too surprising for this exceptional kid to make the transition. But what about all the exceptional kids who don't? How much of the creativity and intelligence of our country's youth lies wasted and untapped? What hope can there be for the average kid growing up in these circumstances? And what of those children whose impairments go beyond their environment?

In working with Gil on this book, I was allowed to help one of our young war refugees be heard. I hope that it allows readers to see the similarities between these children and their own, and I hope that it challenges them to cast aside their notions of grouping urban youth together as unsalvageable and destructive. Grouping people into masses is dangerous. It allows us to discount them. It removes them from our daily life and dehumanizes their problems and rights. But there's a lesson my grandmother used to recite: "The world is like a hand and all the people its fingers. If you hate and destroy one group of people, you lose a finger, and the grasp of the world is less." How much of our grip do we need to lose before we are all crippled? And what can we do to prevent this from happening?

First we have to listen; that's what this book is about. That's what I learned from working with Gil. We can then look at urban youth as being in a situation instead of feeling that they are the situation. In his unique voice, Gil uses this book to inform the reader of the pain and beauty that surrounds him, the hope he has, and the struggle he faces. Please listen to him.

The air in my neighborhood is harder. It's more thicker, harder to breathe in, harder to see through. It's like it's polluted. I don't see stars or nothing. I don't like where I live when I see people on the corner selling drugs, or if there's a shooting, or like when the police has to come out and have a big lineup. Once when my mother

This Is How It's Going Down

was coming out of the store, someone got shot right in front of her.

I want a better lifestyle. I want to be like the kid in *Home Alone.* I was looking at him. He's not really acting. I could do the same thing. He got a chance. I just be thinking to myself, if only I have a chance. But

I will. I will get it. I will have a chance.

That's what I want to tell kids. I know it's hard with peer pressure and all. Keep your head up. I know how it will probably affect you and everything 'cause kids think, "Why should we care? Our parents don't care." Some parents be fooling around, using drugs, not doing things for themselves. They don't care if kids are hungry or staying out all night. But I want to say to kids that if you care for yourself, you're going to be something. No matter if you have a hard time now, you can have a better time later.

I want people who don't come from the neighborhood to know how rough it is, how we have to work hard, and that there's too much pressure, too much violence. If they knew, they would say, "Wow! These people are working so hard, let's help them." Instead, people say, "I heard 'bout your neighborhood, you must be a crackhead." They don't give you a chance.

And people where I come from don't give people from out the neighborhood a chance, either. They think you have it easier, that you don't have to work that hard, that you have it better. They're people who can't see a chance for themselves so they can't give anyone else a chance. There is no understanding.

People feel it has always been the way it is and they can't do nothing about it, but they have to look beyond what they hear and see. They should make it their business to find out. I made that choice, and it gave me freedom.

In the Morning

Like everybody, my day starts with me having to be dragged from the bed that I didn't want to get in the night before. My father wakes me up. He kids me to get me up. He'll, like, play smack me or drop water on my face. If it's really hot, he'll drip cold water on my face. If I'm not moving, he'll raise the television volume—like to Channel 3 with the sssssh noise. If my father didn't wake me up, I'd stay sleeping.

In the morning, the first thing I do is brush my teeth—twice! 'Cause when you're sleeping, that's when your breath stinks the most. I do this with the radio on. My father makes me listen to 1010 WINS news station, 'cause he wants me to be informed. But when I get back into my room, I put on "Howard Stern" or "Good Day New York" on Channel 5.

My father makes me breakfast, like eggs. If it was me, I'd put shrimps in it if I had some. Sometimes he makes waffles, pancakes, or sausage. He's just nice, you know. But I know he hasn't slept, 'cause he watches the building at night. A while ago, people came in and murdered the family upstairs and there was blood dripping down the wall. It was a crack spot. All you heard was POW, POW, POW! They sold drugs; they was involved. So these guys just went off on them. Like eight family members were killed.

Dad wants to protect mom and me. I get to sleep.

On the train to school, I like to be in the first car or the last car, 'cause I want to be outside, not feel like I'm on a train. I do pull-ups or sometimes I dance and do a show, but only if I'm with somebody funny, if the kid has the same personality as me. If the kid I'm with is serious, it's not good to fool around. That's the Bronx. You have to be with it. If the person is serious and

Why People Act That Way

you're joking around, he may take it the wrong way. He might be thinking about something else or a problem that he's having. If he's serious, it's for a reason. I think I know where people are coming from. I think about that before I react.

Teachers at my school won't mess with the seniors, 'cause they feel the seniors don't care. The seniors that are doing bad are ready to drop out. They don't care about teachers. If a kid is having a hard time in school and the teacher tries to get on his case, the student brings his anger to the teacher. To avoid a lot of stuff, the teacher just forgets about it and does not even argue. They may just call security.

My first class is English, so we can fool around. The teacher don't care if we come in late—he said he didn't care. If you finish your work, he gives you a pass. He's always telling us how good he is. Saying, "I'm not going to be like those other teachers. Why should I say you're late or mark you down?" He don't check our homework or nothing. He got beat up last year, so he's different now.

Hanging
with a Friend

You can't trust no one, even your best friend. Things happen so much. There was this kid who came by my house
to pick up his Game Boy. He was like my best friend. So
we went to my room to get it, and the next thing I knew
he had left. He didn't inform me he was leaving. He took
my money, about seven or eight dollars. So now I have to
mess him up.

My father let him out of the house without asking
me, 'cause he figured the kid was my friend. My father
doesn't let people leave the house. He don't want people
just opening the door. It's hard in the 'hood, you know.
A lot of people is bugged out, even people you know.
Certain people live on the second floor, and they do wild
stuff. They just leave the drugs and crack all out. They
don't care if they're your friend, they steal just to provide
for themselves. So my father watches the door. He lets
people in and out.

Maybe I won't fight this kid, 'cause I do feel sorry
for him. His mom is less fortunate. She has to work hard.
She has a lot of children. So he doesn't come out much,
because he doesn't have a lot of clothes. He had to take
the money from my house, 'cause he don't get no money.
The only money he gets is when his mom sends him to
the store, and with the change he'll buy himself something—like a little chocolate. So I used to feel sorry for

him and be his friend. I let him in my house, and he did this to me. I don't know what to do. I could tell him I have to fight him even though I don't want to, because he took my money and all that, but when I think about it, it is hard to decide. The next time I see him, I might fight him. If he beats me up, I'll have to deal with it.

Like Being in Jail

The metal detector don't stop nothing, 'cause the kids bring the weapons in from the back door. Kids open it and let other kids in. Sometimes the guards let kids back in when they shouldn't, 'cause they don't want to be fighting with everyone. The guards try to joke around with the kids and don't always stop them. Kids bring knives, guns, razors, brass knuckles, and stuff like that.

My school is mostly boys—there's not even a girls' bathroom. So there's too much boys. Too much boys have a lot of arguments. So, like 60-something percent, that I know of, bring stuff. There's some I don't know of. That's the quiet ones. They really carry mostly because they're scared. So they can pull out something. That's dangerous, 'cause they react quick, feeling like their life is in danger. If they don't have the ability to fight, or they can't fight, they carry something. They fear the other person, 'cause there are no fair fights now. They could get jumped, or maybe the other person is stronger or has a weapon. So even if you don't want to carry something, you carry something.

I'm not afraid in school, 'cause I know everyone and I don't have a beef with anyone. I had a beef with someone, but that has already been taken care of. I left my hat on a desk, you know, and somebody took it. So it's just something you got to deal with. The kid might not be a thief, but it was just right there, and he took it.

But I don't feel it's dangerous, because I know everyone. They call me "Papichulo." I'm short, and there are people in my class who are nineteen. They look after me, the big kids, 'cause I make them laugh. They snap with me about being short.

The Day Begins
at Third Period

I start at third period, 'cause first period is at 7:30 and I'm not trying that. I have to get up at 6:00 to get there by third period. I take the train or two buses to my school. I don't go to the school by my house, 'cause I know too many people there. At this school, there's something new, something different. I snap with kids while I ride. The time goes fast.

Street Smarts

I went to the store while my father got dinner. People wait at the store when you're buying your food. They say, "Could you give me five dollars and I'll give you five dollars worth of food stamps?" They want to buy drugs, but food stamps ain't money, so they exchange it. Sometimes they'll give you more stamps than money so you can make something on it. Some people just do it so the person with the stamps don't 'cause them any trouble. Nothing bad has ever happened to me, 'cause people know my dad.

People think my father is tough because he has attitude—around the block, anyway. He's a nice guy, but he doesn't kid around with people 'cause a lot of people around my block play with their hands and disrespect

Street
Smarts
Smarts

you. They don't do stuff like that with my dad, 'cause for all the years that he had been there, he kept a serious attitude. He don't feel right around there. If he showed them that he played around, these guys would try stuff. So, every time they see him, he's all serious and stuff. No one messes with him, 'cause he works out and does what he has to do. So when these guys realize that he's over here doing what he has to do, not selling drugs or mess-ing up anything, they take it as, "Wow, this guy's not playing around, so let's not play with him."

My dad wants to be treated the way he treats other people. Where I live at, you know, there are certain peo-ple you have to be serious with; if not, they would do something stupid. Like, he reacts fast. Once, when my father was worried about my mother, he left the house and somebody said, "Hey, what's up?" My father said, "What's up?" and threw his arms up to fight, all serious-like. The guy knew this wasn't a time to mess around.

So, whenever I walk up the block, from, like, the store, a lot of people be looking at me, staring at me. They don't say nothing—maybe one says "hi"— 'cause they know I'm just going to the store to get what I need. I'm serious. That's what I learned from my father. When to be serious.

I Want to Do Something

I want to be a professional basketball player. I want to do something. I just want to be famous. I would live in a house with a built-in basketball court, a full court. I want to give the neighborhood something I would have wanted when I was a kid, that no one ever thought of giving us— like indoor basketball, a batting cage, and a swimming pool. I'd have a sports complex to help people stay out of trouble. I would want to give things to keep minds hopeful. Then kids could say, "Why should I hang out on the corner when I could swim or play basketball?" A lot of kids would like it, but they don't have it.

So kids that can't play baseball outside can go indoors to use the batting cage and practice. Then, when they start to get good at it, they'll start to want to be into sports so they can stay good at it. They would meet friends there and say things like, "This guy's good. You should play him." The peer pressure would change to, like, competition—not drugs and stealing.

If I was famous, I would like to share with the neighborhood the things that helped me.

Told What I Already Knew

My dad said Mom was getting sick. I had figured it out on my own, but didn't say nothing. I was hoping it would go away. But she was losing weight and not doing things the way she used to. She liked the house to be perfect. Now she needed everything done for her. It made me grow up. I want to be more committed to my mom. I think about her now more than myself. I keep hoping that she'll get better, but for now I'll just be with her.

Alexis

My mom named my baby sister Alexis 'cause she liked that name. This lady was named Alexis on the soaps, on *Dynasty*. I remember Alexis even though I couldn't be there for her first and only birthday, 'cause I had the chicken pox. But we videotaped it, so I saw it. It was nice. I got a picture of my mom, my grandmother, my sister, and me from my birthday.

The first time I saw Alexis, when she came home with my mother, I thought, "Wow, I got a sister." But I couldn't hold her or nothing, 'cause she was in an oxygen thing. She was all right for a little while, 'cause I used to always take pictures and snapshots. I used to always bother her. You know, play with her. I know she liked me, 'cause I used to make her laugh. I used to make faces and noises, and she would die laughing. She would laugh like a grown-up. She would throw her head back and laugh hard. Like she knew she had to get all her laughing in quick.

The Brush-off

In art class today, we painted. We're doing water paints now. It's the kind of art class where we learn about different cultures and then do it. But I don't like the teacher. She can't control the class. She's whacked and really old, like fifty, like an antique.

And all of her stuff is from different places. This is from Egypt, this is handmade in China, or this is from England. She pushes it too hard. She brought in this paintbrush from France. She makes us aware that something came from France, so it's good. Like, she'll say,

"This brush is better 'cause all the other brushes are made from horsehair." So, if that brush is better than what we have, we all want it. She transforms this brush into a big thing. She makes us all want it. She says she will give it to someone, but she doesn't bring in brushes for everyone. So the person who gets this good brush will be a better artist, or will be better at whatever she brings in. Every time you think if you have this thing she brings in, you will be better.

Sometimes it's a mystery, like the pyramids, whether the teachers like the kids or not. Sometimes they don't have no feelings. They tell us it's up to us. They say, "If we're going to learn something, you're going to learn it." I think sometimes they care, but I'm not sure. So we snap on the art teacher.

Shout
Out

Today, this kid said, "You want to fight? Come out to the hall." I didn't know why. Some kids just shout you out. So he went to the hall to wait for me. I had to go. But when I went out, I put on this big Kool-Aid smile like Eddie Murphy in *Harlem Nights*. When the kid saw me, he smiled and didn't want to fight, but the class was watching, so we just wrestled. You know, to keep respect. It's the audience thing.

I tried out for the basketball
team, but I messed up 'cause
I was too scared 'cause that's
my favorite sport. It wasn't
that the other kids were
better—a lot of them were
scrubs. When I went, a lot
of people were watching me.
People expected me to get on
it, which was scary. I heard
one kid say, "See that white
kid over there, he's going to
make it." Then I realized he
was talking about me. I'm the
white kid, 'cause my skin is
light and most of the other
kids in school are African
American. Even the other
Spanish kids call me white.
So this kid starts telling
people, "That white kid over
there, he's nice. Watch that
dribble and bounce. You better put the 'D' (Defense) on
him and step on him hard."
That's when I got scared. They
were expecting stuff from me.
I did my foul shots and my
jump shots, but I messed up.
I'll try again.

Basketball Jones

The Hospital

My dad was fixing up the house. You know, cleaning it up and throwing junk out. He asked me to do him a favor and after school go visit my mother in the hospital. I could travel, so it's not a problem. She's not doing well. She had to pee, and a nurse had to come and take her to the bathroom. I stayed with her. I help her out, make her happy if I can. She wanted some juice, so I ran downstairs to get it. I think it's a Jewish hospital, 'cause one Friday they told me I had to hurry because it was almost the Sabbath. After the sun goes down, you're not allowed to buy nothing—at all. My church celebrates the Sabbath, too, but we're Catholic. So I hurried just to make sure and I got her some juice and a piece of fruitcake. She ate pretty good, but I had to feed her. Later I fed her her dinner, some chicken, some potatoes, and some carrots. The phone was working and the TV, too. So it was good.

When the nurse dressed her, she put her shirt on backwards. When I saw it, I was bugging out 'cause I know how my Mom is. She likes me to be perfect. Sometimes I do things correct but not perfect. She likes me to do it perfect, so I knew she wasn't happy about this shirt thing. So I dressed her, but we didn't talk. It was a silent thing between us.

I made my mother laugh about the nurse being funny-looking. She was cold, so I got her a blanket from the nurse. She asked me where it came from so I teased her. Told her the patient next door went to the bathroom so I grabbed it quick. She laughed and said, "I hope this person's not sick." "I think, Mom, if he is in the hospital, something has to be wrong with him." Then I teased her by putting it over her face. She screamed, "Gil take it down! I don't know what this person's got." Then I told her it was a joke, and she laughed.

I know all the nurses and doctors there now and I help them take care of my mom and stuff. I make sure she takes her medicines; I even give them to her. I also keep my eye on that drip bag thing.

Talking Shop

The shop teacher lost the final he made up so he gave us the midterm test again. I knew what I got wrong the last time so I aced it. Some of the older kids wanted to cheat off me, but I told them I didn't study and was guessing. They left me alone. Some of them ask people for money, but I don't have that problem 'cause they like that I'm funny. They say I'm not a pest and they can have fun with me. Mostly it's 'cause I'm a positive-type person. I'm funny, I think about creative things, and I have a good sense of humor. They don't have to worry about if I'm going to ask them for this or that or that I'll want to borrow money. They don't have to look out for me or say, "Watch out he's going do this, like steal or snitch."

I make them laugh. Like this one big guy in my class, I tell him I may have to mess him up. He laughs and says, "This kid's bugging out." So I says, "Did I tell you to talk! Who said you could talk?" He laughs again, so I ask him, "Do you want me to beat you up now or later? That's it, no video games for you!"

Government Food

At lunch in the cafeteria, there are about ten hundred people waiting to go through one door. When it finally opens, you have to stick your ID through the machine so they don't mark you for cutting. The teachers walk around and tell you to take off your hat so they can see your face. We get in line again for food, but I wait 'cause it's too long. So I wait and sit down and tell my friends I'll wait till it gets short. But it seems to grow, looks like it's getting longer. So I get in line and hand in my tickets for food. The tickets are different colors for chicken, fruit, and fries, but you have to pay ten cents for milk. There is a snack bar with cookies, cake, candy, and stuff, but you have to pay for it extra.

It's fun to sit around with the boys and talk. We snap on each other, dis the teachers, or laugh about the food. The food is so bad I'd rather wait on the welfare line for government cheese. These cafeteria ladies cook the stuff, but I don't think they eat it. They seem to cook whatever they have, 'cause they've never asked the students what they want.

For Christmas they give you a holiday cookie, for Thanksgiving a cookie, for African American History Month a cookie . . .

Call Me
Air Alicea

I like to pretend I'm someone else when I put on my basketball jersey. I use other people's names, depending on what I'm doing. If I'm dribbling, Tim Hardaway; if I'm an all-around player, Michael Jordan; if I'm shooting, Chris Mullin; and if I'm going to dunk up, Shawn Kemp. If I'm in a slam-dunk competition, I think Jordan.

I like thinking to myself that 'cause my last name is Alicea it sounds better to be Air Alicea. I feel better about playing. I feel like I got to dunk just like Jordan. I try to think like him. When I'm being Michael, I even stick out my tongue like him. I do the moves of whoever I'm doing. If I'm Shawn Kemp, I would play like him. He's tall, which I can't do. But he keeps his arms up and out around his waist, so he's ready for anything. That I can do. If I'm Tim Hardaway, I play low. He dribbles low, that's how he passes. If I'm Jordan, I just go up. I take the ball around my back or put it through my legs. I think about all the players' moves.

But if I'm playing as myself, I use my shortness. I dribble on my knees, and they're taller and can't get down there. Then the kids say, "You're playing good—you keep it up and you're going to be real good." I have this move that I would dribble on my knees and bring the ball around the other side. People use their height as an advantage. I use my shortness as an advantage.

Grandma: Seventy Going On Twenty

After school, I go to the store, do the dishes, fix up the cabinets. Dad likes it when I hook up the kitchen. He appreciates it and says it to me. I may go see my grandmother depending on if she cooked for us or needs money or something. My grandmother is old but with a young heart, 'cause she likes doing a lot of stuff. She cleans and cooks.

She makes this chicken with special seasoning. The skin of the chicken is red. It's great. But I'm not used to her cooking. She makes the nastiest

Girl Talk

You know my school is mostly boys. So I spend all day mostly looking at boys. When I get home and see girls I say, "Oh man, am I hallucinating?" I met this one girl, but she couldn't give out her number 'cause she's Catholic school and all that. Her parents are strict. She can't be talking to boys on the phone. She invited me to a party so I could talk with her.

I impress girls by being myself. Like a girl knows that I'm funny. They like that. Being funny and smart is the way to a girl's heart. But if you want them to like you, just be yourself. If the girl likes you, there's something about you she likes. So don't be a faker. 'Cause if she likes you and you're a faker, you can never be yourself around her and never be comfortable. You always feel you have to put on this act just to please her. She don't like you, she likes the act she thinks you are.

I talk to girls about whatever they want to talk about. I don't try to talk about only what I want to talk about, like sports. Girls are good at talk. They talk, talk, talk. They talk about everything, like clothes and music. They know about everything. They can talk about one subject for hours. Like, if they're saying a match fell on the floor, they mention how it fell, if it flipped, or did it bounce off the floor. You know, they tell you all the details.

the

Last period of the week is math. I call my
teacher "Big Bird" 'cause he's too tall. He
covers the whole blackboard. He's white and lives in
Middletown. Most of the teachers live upstate, not in the
neighborhood. Like they're worried someone is going to
follow them home or something. He tries to make us
laugh. It's like a class of jokes. He lets the kids snap each
other for a little while to relax us. He understands that
since there is mostly boys in the school, we'll be a little
wild. There are only about fifty girls, because it's a trade
school. Not many girls want to be draftsmen, carpenters,
or auto-body mechanics. So my math teacher lets us mess
up—for a few minutes.

Math

33
...

My Dad

At home, my father teaches me how to survive, how to do
things correctly in life, and just take care of myself. But
he also says, "Be a kid. Don't grow up too fast, 'cause
that's what I did." Everyone wants to be an adult just to
see what it's like. But my father, now that he's grown up,
he wants to be a kid.

The Day of Rest

On Saturday, I go to church from 9:00 a.m. to 10:00 p.m. This man named Richie picks me and a bunch of kids up in his van. He's a doctor. We go to mass for four hours in the morning. At mass, people talk, sing, and tell stories. I sit but I don't always listen. I may talk to a friend sometimes—about Jesus, of course.

Later, we go downstairs to eat together in a big group. It makes me feel good. These people in the kitchen cook the food: chicken, pasta, and rice and beans. On Saturday, we're not supposed to buy anything 'cause it's the Sabbath. 'Cause in the Bible it says that Fridays are for working and Saturdays are for rest. After we eat, we relax, hang out, and talk. Then more Mass.

The preacher speaks Spanish, so I only understand some of it. We sing in Spanish, too. So if I don't understand, I just move my lips. The singing sounds good and gives me strength. Later we go back downstairs and do Bible studies, have celebrations, or do plays as each other. At the Pathfinders, there's also a merit thing. You get badges for stuff.

People at church look out for you. I was walking home with a friend, and we had our ties on and all that. I had my jacket open, and my friend said, "Put your jacket up." I said, "Why?" "'Cause you have a tie and all that on. People will know you just came from church and consider you a herb and they'll take your jacket." A herb is a punk. So I closed my jacket.

Visiting Mom

I know now about the silent thing that happens when I help my mother get dressed. I don't feel it's the time to talk. It's like something I had to do for her. She can't do it on her own. I have to help her and all that. She must be thinking, "I should be doing this. The littlest thing, getting dressed is something that I want to do but can't." A lot of stuff is being taken away, which hurts her. What could we say while I'm dressing her?

I try to make my mother happy. I tell her not to worry and I talk about God. She likes that. I say, "Don't worry. Jesus is with you at all times and will be with you no matter what. He's coming, but some people who love him have to suffer." I kiss her. I make her feel that she's loved. I do faces or dances to make her laugh. Like I lip-sync to old songs: "I found love on a one-way street and lost it on a lonely highway." Then I do these movements. She laughs.

But I worry that if, God forbid, she passes away, she won't be ready. I'm very religious, so I think that Jesus is going to come. But you know a lot of people think different—and when I say "think" I mean "believe." There are different theories. I believe in my religion. That's my belief. I'm into that, so I tell my mother this stuff to get her ready, because I'm positive this is true. I want her to be ready, if she passes away, and someday I will be with her in heaven for eternity.

Night Moves

I have all my clothes for the week ready on Sunday night. So, during the week, I know what I'm going to wear. I'll wear this on Monday, this on Tuesday. My dad tells me I don't have to, but I want to look nice. I want to match.

Bad Deal

The cops were told not to get the small dealers, but I think any drug dealer you could lock up is great. Jails is, like, packed. They think if they got big people on the top, they're taking away a lot of people. But all the people working for that big dealer is too spread out. So if you get each of them, little by little, and the big guys, you have less to worry about.

Legalizing drugs is a bad thing. Then kids will say "Ah! It's not against the law!" People will just be on the street with needles getting high. More people freaked out, suicides, murders. 'Cause the drugs today make you act second-rate. So you don't know what's up. You're paranoid, you know.

When
Alexis
Left

Alexis passed when I was eleven. It was sad, but I really
didn't understand. 'Cause she was sick, I hadn't been
really, really close to her. I didn't know what it was to
miss her. My parents were sad, and it was hard in my
house for a while. We had to get money for the funeral
'cause it was expensive. And two weeks before that my
grandmother had passed. I was close to her. I had been
crying a lot. I tried not to think about it, but I missed her.
It was hard to talk to my parents at that time, 'cause they
were thinking about my grandmother and Alexis. I don't
know, but it was like all the sadness was used up, but it
was still there.

Getting
Through

To get through, kids do different things. One kid said,
"Yo Gil, me and this kid went to Macy's and we had these
Super Nintendo games in our shirts and in our pants and
all that. We was walking out but there was a camera and
I didn't know if the camera saw us. Tomorrow you want

to come with us?" I said no. He's crazy 'cause I don't want to live like that. I have stuff and I don't really want something that bad to face the consequences later. I can't say it was worth it. If I want something, I just ask my dad and if he says no, he says no. He would get it for me if he could.

I knew someone, he was in my grade, but he got involved. He don't be around the block, 'cause people want to kill him and the police want to catch him. He's a hideout, with no place to go.

Kids like me play sports and video games or flip basketball cards. This is what's fun for me 'cause I don't worry about getting caught. I don't have to be scared that someone finds out. You have to be sneaking 'round your parents. But me, I don't have to worry about anything. I'm having fun. This gives me freedom.

I made a choice, but a lot of kids don't have a lot of stuff. There's no food in the house. They got no clothes or games. So they don't have a choice. They feel stealing the stuff is worth it. School isn't going to give them money or clothes. That's how they think. They say, "I'm not going to school. I'll just cut 'cause I don't have no good clothes to go to school. What I have is dirty, ripped, filthy. I don't have this game and everybody has a game." Their parents set bad examples, using drugs, so how could these kids see a future?

Step by Step

I think about the future a lot. What I'm going to do. Not
way in the future. I think about that sometimes, but I
think about what I'm going to do in an hour from now,
two hours from now. I'm going to do this or that. I
always think about today. Let tomorrow be tomorrow
and let yesterday be yesterday, but think about today,
'cause it's what I'm going to do. I feel comfortable 'cause
I know what I'm going to be doing. So I have everything
planned, so I'll be on schedule. Like I'm going to do this
or this. 'Cause if I'm off schedule, it turns out messed up
for me.

My dad, when I didn't clean my room, he used to
give me a schedule. He said, "At 2:00 p.m., you go outside. Come in at 4:00, eat, go back outside for an hour,
and then this time come in and take a shower, eat, and
do your room and all that stuff." That's how come I think
about it. I think it's good, 'cause you could be doing anything you want to be doing and not be on somebody
else's schedule. You're always on your schedule and know
how you're going to do something. When I pick out my
schedule, it's better for me. I learned from my father, but
I do it 'cause I feel it's good.

Sometimes I go off my schedule. Like if I'm outside I think I'm going to stay outside for another half hour. I just say it to myself and do it. So if I tell my dad I'm coming back at 8:00 p.m., then outside I feel like I'm having more fun, I say I got a half-hour bloop to play with. You can rearrange your schedule for your own good, but it's still good to have one. I know most kids don't have schedules, 'cause I see my friends. They don't know what to do. They'll play basketball, but they don't know what to do next. They sit down for a while. So I see them and I say, "You want to play?" And they say, "Hold on, hold on." It's like they are thinking what to do next. And then, finally, they can go do something. It takes them time to think about it.

Like for me, if I'm playing basketball, after I'm going someplace else—I'm going to my house or wherever—I know I'm going to do it 'cause I made time. It's just that a lot of my friends don't think about schedules. They just say, "I'm maybe going to play basketball." To me it's nothing bad, you could do that, but it's better to be on a schedule. 'Cause it makes me stay in control. My friends don't have that.

It's better for my dad to know what I'm going to do, too. I tell him I'm going to do this and come in at this time. That way he feels more comfortable 'cause he knows what I'm up to. He's not going to be guessing,

"Oh, where's Gil?" Sometimes I just want to stay outside all day, just playing basketball, but I got a schedule. It's helpful for me and my dad. 'Cause he knows I'm not doing anything bad, and if I'm on schedule I won't.

I Want to Be

When I go outside to play basketball, I have different uniforms from different teams. Like Starks on the Knicks, Jordan on the Bulls, and Barcelona. I even have one from the Le Parker Meridien Hotel. It's a nice outfit. It has the shorts and it looks nice, you know, with the shirt and jersey. Plus the practice shirt and all that. It's like I can be on all the teams. So I look like I'm really going to play. Everybody can tell that, too.

Nonstop

I been messing up. I haven't been playing basketball the way I used to because I overtrained recently. I just played basketball all the time, nonstop, nonstop. I just started to feel weak and tired, like exhausted. My leg is bad. I went to the doctor and he gave me the name of some problem. I have to go back.

It's Not Going to Be Me

Dad tells me to learn from other people's mistakes. Like when I see my friends or someone using drugs. I see they look messed up. Like my friends who used to play basketball real, real good. They started to use drugs and get really messed up. Now they can't even get a foul, 'cause they cry or fight about it or something. I see how they act and all that and I know drugs are bad. So that right there says why would I want to feel like them?

But kids see this and use drugs anyway, 'cause they want to be cool. To hang out and everything, just to see how it feels. If all these people are doing it, they say, "Hey, let me try it." Then they say, "I'm not going to get addicted. I'm not going to be smoking crack all my life." They see other people addicted, but they don't learn from other people. It's easy for me 'cause I see it. Not because my parents told me. But they don't see it. They have to be cool.

Coppers

All the kids around where I live think the cops are bad
'cause they're always running from them. Older kids think
the cops are bad, so all the kids think the cops are bad.
It's just that they think the cops do bad things, even if
they don't see them do bad things. You can't hang out or
talk with them, 'cause the kids think you're a snitch. You
could get hurt, too, 'cause, "snitches get stitches." And
the cops never talk to the kids, never even try. So, when,
like, all those cops got arrested for drugs, the kids say
they're all messed up. So we don't think about the cops.
We don't take them serious. But since all those cops got
caught, it says they're sneaky, too. The kids always
thought it.

Seeing All the Violence Start

When I was young, I used to watch the karate stuff on TV.
Then I would go outside and want to do it. The other kids
around my way would do it, too. We would see the karate
guy beat everyone, and we want to do that, too: to do his
moves, walk on air, land on spikes and not die. You don't
worry about getting hurt or nothing, 'cause people in the
movie don't get hurt. Like Ninja Stars, they're like these
disks with sharp edges. You buy them at the Chinese

stores. I used to buy them. I got caught once in school and got suspended. We used to throw them at trees. I didn't think about getting hurt or not getting hurt. I just did it. I wanted to be a karate master, so people would know I knew martial arts. But when I got older, I realized I could get hurt or hurt someone else. I don't think television violence is bad if you're older and understand. But when you're little, you don't understand. You have to inform kids.

Like I used to think wrestling was real. They hit each other with chairs and stuff, but nobody gets hurt. Somebody wins, but nobody gets hurt. You even see a small guy beat up a big guy. So you think if you fight that way, you could beat a big guy, 'cause it looks real. When I was young, I thought everything on television was real. I thought it was happening at that moment. Even if I saw a commercial two times. I would watch to see if the person could do the same expression again. I was only seven or eight, and my friends thought this, too—that what was happening on TV was really happening.

It's bad for kids to think TV's true. Parents have to explain this to kids, but they're not always there to inform them that everything you see is not true. I know that if I was a parent, I would teach this. But some kids and parents don't even talk to each other. Maybe school could teach that lesson, too. The TV could maybe explain before the show that the stuff or fighting on TV isn't real. If they want kids to stay alive, they would.

Learning Sensation

Beakman's World is a television show I like 'cause it's fun and teaches you things about sciences. This show taught me about all the veins in the body. Like, did you know if you stretched them all out, you could go around the world twice? Twice around the whole world and they're right in your body. Imagine that. Kids like learning about wild things, especially the things this show teaches. It got my attention. They taught how to make a rocket. It teaches you by showing you how things work. It's hip.

Good-bye Mom

Afterwards I just prayed. I would talk to her in my prayers. I say stuff like, "Now that you're along with my little sister and taking care of her, don't worry about me. I'm doing okay. Watch over me. I'm going to see you and everything."

One Day at a Time

My dad thinks about my mom a lot. My dad is hurting a lot. He be stressing out. That's all that be on his mind. It's there before he goes to sleep and the first thing when he wakes up. So, it's the first and last thing, and everything between the days, he be thinking about her.

I try not to think about it too much 'cause I know that I'm going to miss her. It's better to think about her along with good things, but sometimes it's hard. I just keep myself busy. That's what I do. I play Genesis, or play with my basketball hoop in my house. I have a full basketball thing right in my room, with a rubber ball that's like a balloon. It's just like a basketball, but it doesn't bounce hard. It has a battery for a score, time clock, and shooting contest. I ask a friend to come over and play just to stop thinking about mom.

I try to do the same thing for my dad, try to keep him busy. I do stuff with him, like just talk to him so he won't be there thinking by himself. Just talking to him has his mind being busier right there, or I watch a game with him. We talk about the moves and which player is the best. We always argue, 'cause he says this guy from the Nets, Derrick Coleman, that no one could beat him. No one in basketball, in fighting or nothing. I keep telling him there's too many big guys that could mess Coleman up, that are just too big for him. My dad says that

Shaquille O'Neal is young and Coleman will tear him up inside. But there's too many. They got Charles Barkley, Larry Johnson, and Karl Malone. Dad's always picking a player that you wouldn't think he would say, 'cause he sees them on commercials.

It's good to keep my father busy about other things. 'Cause even though he's stressed out, he can laugh about basketball or watch the fights or wrestling. I challenge him to basketball in my room. I make him laugh 'cause I say, "You can't beat me." So he says, "Wait till you're older and you might probably be able to score on me."

48

The Media
Takes It
to the Extreme

The news always trying to be in your business. They try
to suck up any little thing that they think you hiding or
just trying to find out something because they think if
they're not pushing you they're not doing their job. So
they think they have to find out all your problems and
everything. If you do something, like Michael Jordan did,
they make it a problem. He was in a casino, gambling a
little, just to have fun, 'cause he was stressed out from
the playoffs. So he wanted a break. He went to the casino,
you know, 'cause he wanted to gamble a little. The next
thing, they took it all out of proportion. "That Michael
Jordan, he's a gambler. He wastes all his money. He gam-
bled this amount of money and stayed up till three
o'clock in the morning, even though he have a game."
They should let him do what he wants to do. If he wants
to do that, let him do that. What's the big deal? He can't
even go to the movie theater without a hundred people
following him with questions. It's bad enough that where
he lives he can't go to a high-class restaurant.

When I read what they say about him, I say, "Wow,
it's like he has to be perfect." If he wants to do something he has to hide it. He can't do it freely. He is always
looked at differently. But nobody is perfect. The media
takes it to extremes. Now he's like a big role model, so

anything he does affects the children or affects how the people look at him. I think that if he scores sixty-four points in a game, the press should say "Michael Jordan did good. He's a great basketball player." But they say "Michael Jordan scored sixty-four points, but didn't you see him at the casino at twelve midnight?" It's like they owned him or something. They do it to his parents, too. He cannot even do what he wants to do. They should focus on the good stuff, not the bad. It's like they want to get him because he's a role model. Only he still is one.

School: Not by the Book

I got this book of schools from the Board of Education to pick a new school. It was broken down by boroughs. I saw the pictures from Staten Island, Queens, Manhattan, and Brooklyn. They were pictures of kids studying, doing their work, looking happy and quiet, even doing ballet, but the picture from the Bronx was the worst. It had kids with boomboxes all in a bunch, screaming and yelling with their arms raised and looking all rowdy. It's like they told the kids, "Get in a big bunch and scream." Someone decided that! They didn't tell the kids from Queens or Manhattan to do that. With us it was different. It's a Board of Education book, and they did this. You can imagine the issues they have if they think this way.

It makes me feel that a lot of people judge us before we start. You can't win, 'cause first you have to prove them wrong. Other kids don't have to prove themselves first. Why should we prove ourselves? Why can't we start like everybody else? Why we got to be different? Why do we have to be considered wilder than other kids? 'Cause there are bad things going around where we live, all the kids should suffer?

I would change these pictures. They didn't state we're wild in the explanations, but they showed it with the pictures. A picture is worth a thousand words. You don't have to be a genius to notice it. It's like the Board of Education didn't think this was wrong. They have this opinion. It's what they expect, 'cause no matter who took the picture, they picked it.

The Gil Style

I have different styles. Like jeans, nice shirt with a tie, and a cap. It's the casual Manhattan style. It makes me feel good clean. Then there's a dressy shirt, pants, sneakers, and natural look hair. Or a shirt with a vest and comfortable shoes.

My style is like that. Part dressy, part casual. It makes me feel comfortable. It makes me look nice. I feel intelligent. I feel good about myself. I'm not ashamed. I can walk up in anyplace and not worry about nothing

'cause I'm dressed. If I don't have a jacket, I have a vest.
I can go anywhere dressed like this. I don't have to be
looked at different.

This is my own style. I choose it. My style is rare,
unless you're going to church. This style is not harsh.
Anyone can look nice in my style, not just me.

Being Materialistic Is Not Everything

Kids who don't have stuff look at kids who do and feel
that to have a life they have to look nice. They see it on
TV, or from music and sports figures. Kids from rich families and poor families are the same. There's no difference,
except rich kids have money to get what they want.
That's why some kids rob. They think robbing is okay
'cause they get away with it.

Being materialistic is okay, until you feel you got to
have something you can't—you feel you need it. People
believe that if they don't have a certain type of sneakers
or pants, that their whole life ends there. That they can't
go outside anymore. Especially for a holiday or the first
day of school. On the first day of school you have to have
new sneakers and new clothes. You have to. It's mandatory.
I don't know why or where it comes from, but it's the way
it is! So some kids feel a lot of pressure to have things
they can't afford.

The news shows projects burnt down
or messed up with garbage everywhere. Like this reporter
who came to take pictures. He was telling me to go
through these fields to show all the garbage. So people
see the pictures he took and say, "Wow." He told me to
walk through this street that I would never walk down in
my life and dribble my basketball. He thought it would
be good. Why would it be good for people to see garbage
on the floor, fields of dirt, and stripped cars in the background? Why not show the good parts? If I'm living here,
why do I have to go to this block, that I would never in
my life go to, and take pictures? I just let it be.

The press looks at people from my neighborhood
as being in gangs, not good with money, house messed
up, drugged, and a lot of bad stuff. They show people not
having anything, not being organized, or always being
behind on things. If they do show something good, it has
to be great. 'Cause if they show people just living happy,
they say, "Forget about that. It's only once in a blue
moon." Or they think that someone is trying to prove
something or impress, not being real.

Like the reporter asked me what would I do with
money—buy a pair of sneakers? I thought, a pair of sneakers,
what are you talking about? It's kind of dumb. They always
have a picture in their head before they do their story. I
have other things to think about than a pair of sneakers.

It's like the press thinks everyone where I live is the
same. They put us in a category, and that's where we stay.

Why
would
it be
good
for people
to see
garbage
on
the floor
fields of
dirt
and
ripped
cars in the
background?

Why
not
show the
good parts?

We're not going to move up, 'cause the press wants us to stay in that category and not hear any ifs or buts about it. It's negative, 'cause they think everyone is doing everything wrong just 'cause some people do.

If a news show comes to where I live, it's to put more dirt on our grave. Just to tell people, "Look at this problem or that problem."

A Coin for Your Thoughts

I started a coin collection. I have foreign coins from Iran, Russia, and the Dominican Republic. It's fun to collect things and you have a little bit of everything. You won't get bored 'cause you have things to learn about. You can even get books to learn more about the stuff you have. Now I have new things to talk about with friends or anybody. I have more to talk about than if I'm doing the usual things. It's like, now that I have different interests, that I can share. Other people will want to share their interests with me.

Spike: The Real Deal

New Jack City was full of gangs and bangs and, at the end, this guy gets killed. That's all. Drugs, action, blacks and Puerto Ricans, and projects, and that's all. Not just drugs, but big drugs. Of course, they put it where we're at. They're not going to put it in our neighborhood. A lot of these movies don't look at us as individuals. It's not true of everyone, but the gangs and kids is all they know.

Spike Lee I like 'cause he just shows some problems, but then he'll show people having fun in their house. He won't show only big drugs. He'll show, like, issues in the house. He'll also show minor problems. Like in *Crooklyn,* there's a scene where the kids are watching TV upstairs, and the mom downstairs asks, "Is that TV on?" And the three kids are all watching the TV, but yell, "No." It's funny and all that. It's real, 'cause life, even in bad situations, is not all about drugs. It shows more things than the issues movies push like drugs, sex, and killing. It shows just how life is. Shows problems that occur in every household.

Spike doesn't push it and make it like someone just says, "I got some problem or I'm angry, I'm going to smoke some crack now." He shows people care about other people. He understands 'cause he lived in Brooklyn, so he could come out with the real deal. It's like he looked at all the movies and said, "I'm going to do it the right way." That's why his movies make money. We go to see them 'cause the stuff is true. Not just from my block, but from a lot of other blocks. He shows that not everybody in poor neighborhoods don't care for each other. But when people from my block go to the movies, they see only bad things about themselves.

I don't know why they make these negative movies, but I'm not going to judge them 'cause I don't want to be judged.

A Song for a Bad Day

I'm so sad.

One day, will I have a place to go to?

I'm so sad, so sad, so sad.

I wish that I had someone to talk to.

I'm so alone. I wish I had someone.

I wish I could fly.

One day I will have a real friend

Who will understand the feelings
I'm going through,

Who I could talk to because
I'm so sad. I'm so sad.

A Little Bit
About Everything

I want to learn about the ocean, space, everything. So then I could try everything 'cause I don't know what the next life is. I don't even know if there's another life where I can do the things I can here. I want to enjoy it now 'cause maybe I won't be able to later. You got to take the chance when it's yours.

A lot of people just want to stick to the same things because they feel they know what they're doing and are uncomfortable when they don't. So people aren't open. They have fears or bad attitude. A good attitude has you being outgoing and wanting to learn.

I store knowledge I get for the future. I don't know if I'll need it, but I still want it 'cause it's better for me. I feel better each time I learn a new thing. I feel good about myself, that I could learn and remember it. Otherwise I would be bored. I wish there were even more options. So do other kids, but they don't have options. So it makes it easier to hang out and do drugs. You want to try drugs out 'cause it's different. They think it's just one try, but it's never one try.

The Egyptian Belief

At The Metropolitan Museum of Art, they had all these things from years and years ago in Egypt. They were like a mystery. I saw the Temple of Dendur. I learned that these people were very smart. They knew how to put these huge stones so high. They had to work hard. We have machines to do these things and without them we wouldn't know how to move things, but they didn't. They figured out how to move these huge stones without machines. So if we didn't have machines, we would have to learn from them.

They had pictures; they drew on stones and told stories. They believed in a lot of gods. Maybe they knew things that we didn't know. They wrote their alphabet on their walls, about spirits and gods. Maybe all they believed was true. Look at the pyramids. We don't even know how they did it. Maybe they got help from a higher power. Some people said they got so smart, they built ships and went to other planets. It's a mystery. The mystery part is what makes it exciting.

Do Your Best
'Cause
We're Put to the
Test!

You're always put to the test for something. Are we better than someone, better at making something or whatever it is? If you do something and it goes bad, people can say, "That's no surprise. I knew he couldn't do it." But at some time in your life, something you do will go bad. So if it's not right then and there, it's going to be in the future. Something is going to happen and someone may be expecting you to do bad. So kids feel this pressure from adults.

I say, don't worry what people think, it's yourself. It's what you think of yourself, not what other people think. 'Cause if you have low esteem, you'll always be thinking you're doing something bad. But if you feel good about yourself and someone says different, it doesn't matter. You know it in your heart.

Interested in Learning

Steve Cohen, another writer who works with my agent, introduced me to his friend, Barry. He said he would take me fossil hunting. Before I went, I went to Barry's house. It's like a museum—more than a museum. He's got a human brain in a jar, armor, glowing glass, monster masks, and a bunch of rocks. He also does this project with virtual reality, which is this machine with glasses that takes you inside of places.

He had everything. There was even more stuff in the basement. Like this chain-and-rope thing to practice mountain climbing. I thought he had a lot of interests, which is good, 'cause I have a lot of interests. It made me think that I could ask him about the interests I have and he could show me. He gave me a dolphin bone from a hundred million years ago.

I never thought there were so many things to learn about and collect. Like monkey bones, shark teeth, swords, bows and arrows, and darts. He had a lot of crazy stuff. I thought it was good he was doing all these things. I want to do all that.

I think kids know there's a lot of things to do but there's no one to show them. Kids like science, but in school it's just books and the kids don't understand it. But to see it is something else.

School
of Hard Rocks

Barry and I went to New Jersey looking for fossils. Barry
picked me up in a van and we took the Garden State
Parkway for an hour. It didn't surprise me that an hour
from my house things looked so different, 'cause I've
seen how different it can be just a few minutes away. We
went to these mountains to find these fossils. It wasn't
hard to climb, 'cause they weren't steep. So we just
walked up this mountain that was full of trees and rocks.
There's a certain spot with a whole bunch of rocks. For
fossil hunting you need gadgets. Like we had to put this
cream on our clothing so the ticks wouldn't get us.

You have to break the rocks to look for dinosaur
tracks and insect prints. The rock was on the floor, like a
floor of rock. It was an area full of stone and, depending
on how you work, it could take some time. Some people
just turn the stone over. You have to put a bunch of chis-
els around an area, then you hit with a sledgehammer.
After the rock cracks, you lift it and look. This part was
hard. We broke a lot of rocks and didn't find things. I
must have broken like three hundred pounds before I
found one fossil.

We found these tracks from millions and millions
of years ago. The bugs and dinosaurs used to walk
through the mud, which piled up for years and years.

So this dinosaur would step in the mud, it would dry, and the print is left there. I was saying to myself, "This is from millions and millions of years ago and I have it in my hands." I thought that no one was there at that time and now I'm holding this print. I took this dinosaur print the size of a book home. I don't know what kind of a dinosaur it was, but it had three long toes.

It was interesting, but I missed with the hammer and messed up my finger. It really hurt, but when I showed it to Barry, he just said, "I have a load of those." It made me happy to do new things. It was even okay to get injured, 'cause I could say I lost my nail fossil hunting. So now I have a story to tell. I feel I accomplished something.

One Floor at a Time

When I was younger, I used to play with my friends in the elevator. Of course it wasn't my idea. I don't think like that. Now that I have other interests like basketball and writing, it seems dumb. I understand now what could have happened, but when I was younger I did things just 'cause they were something different or it seemed fun.

We used to take the elevator up to the seventh floor. In the elevator, you could press the button and the doors would open, even in between floors. Then you could put a rope around the door and close the door. After the elevator left, you could yank the rope and the door would open. You could see the elevator going down. So we just used to slide down the cable and ride the top of the elevator back up. There would be like this buzzing noise. Then there's this weight thing that goes up as the elevator goes down. We would sit on the bars and ride up with the weight. You had to jump on the elevator from the weight or you could get smashed.

Once my friend jumped, but his shirt got caught and he was just hanging there as the elevator came up. Luckily, someone had pressed the second floor, so me and my other friend had time to pull him up. It was real scary, but we did it again anyway. It was like getting hurt didn't matter.

We used to hold on the back of buses and slide behind them. The cars had to watch, 'cause you could slip off. Sometimes we would ride between subway cars. I look at the younger kids doing this today and think how stupid they are. But I understand why they do it. I used to think that if someone dared you to do something, you had to do it; or I thought if everyone else was doing something, you had to do it. Now I realize I should be doing things 'cause I want to do them. Nobody else has to like it, and I don't have to do what they like. It's not about fitting in anymore.

h. Everybody
knows where my
on is. Their
en
dont
watch
ther

Time to
Pay the
Piper

Outside my friends be teasing me. "It's about that time
that your dad's going to call you in, right? By the summer he'll be getting a bullhorn." Their parents don't
watch them like my dad does me. He's just making sure I
don't do anything bad. You know, like on the news when
they say, "It's 10:00 p.m. Do you know where your children are?" Whenever my dad sees that, he says, "Yeah.
Everybody knows where my son is." He knows that the
other kids have been teasing me about it. He's, like, over-
protective 'cause he thinks I'll be influenced even though
I tell him I'll be okay. But he asks me, "Why do you have
to be out so late?" I don't have a reason.

I know he's right that I can be influenced. I was
with my friend in shop class, and we found this stairway
that no one knew about. It was weird, 'cause there were
these lockers by the staircase. My friend had a hammer,
and he went down the stairs. I went upstairs to see if
anyone was coming, and when I came back, my friend
had broke the locks with the hammer and said, "Look
how easy this was." Then he started to do another one,
but there was a teacher nearby and he caught us.

I only went down the staircase to see what was there. My friend had the hammer, but I had given it to him. He said he was going to break the locks, so I gave it to him. It was like a dare. I didn't think I would get in trouble. I didn't even think he would do it. It was kind of exciting, until he really did it.

We both got into trouble, but I didn't tell my dad. I hoped he wouldn't find out. One morning, I was eating breakfast with my Walkman on, so I didn't hear the phone. It was my school, and my dad got the call. Dad came into the kitchen all mad and said I'm punished. I couldn't do anything but stay in my room until he said. I couldn't go out all weekend.

I know he was right, but I didn't liked getting punished. But I learned something: Don't do crazy stuff. Think about it first, 'cause if you don't think about it, you could do something really stupid. That's why he still watches me.

Good for Some, But Not All

The school I go to now, Smith, has things like carpentry, engineering, and drafting. It's a great school if you look forward to being a carpenter or electrician or that type of stuff, 'cause it offers you a job when you're finished in one of those trades. So it's good if you want to be in those trades, but it's not for me. I want to do business and not mechanics or fixing things. I think those are good jobs, but I don't want to work with my hands. I want to work with my brain.

It will be different in a different type of school, 'cause it will be more interesting to me. Now, when I take all these shop classes, I don't look forward to school 'cause it's not what I want to do. I like different things than working with my hands 'cause that's not really my talent. My talent—I got a few—is like acting, writing, and just talking. That's what I want. A class where you express your thoughts and ideas and all that. It asks you to think about certain issues. A school like that offers you something for your brain.

I went to Smith first 'cause I didn't know much about it. I didn't know much about what I liked, either. Now I know what my talents are, so I'm looking for that. I do want my new school to have a basketball team, too. I know no school has everything, so it doesn't have to be a school known for basketball, as long as it has a team. Then I could have some fun, too.

Scared of Knowing

My dad and I went to Jacoby Hospital for my knee. We had to wait and we started to get scared, 'cause the area was just leg injuries. So when we first walked in the waiting room, everybody had, like, big toe, one leg broke, casts, wheelchairs, or leg braces. My dad kept teasing me: "Yeah, this is the place for you, Gil." Then I heard the sound of a drill and a saw. I thought they were drilling someone's leg, but my dad told me that's how they take off casts. I thought I was going to be messed up like these people.

While we were waiting, they asked my dad to come into this other area and help this other lady who needed someone who spoke Spanish. He had to translate for the doctor. So we knew everything about this lady and all the pain she had for many years. She had this pain in her stomach for, like, ten years, but just came in now. We got to help, which was good.

Then the doctor came to see us. He made my dad and I stand up and put our backs together. My dad whispered, "Now the Doctor's going to say something intelligent." Then the doctor said "Oh, yeah. When Gil gets to your height, this problem will stop." He told me that it's just that I'm growing and my thighs, legs, and calves are growing different. When I grow to my father's height, everything will be even.

I was happy 'cause I could still play basketball, but now I have to stretch before I play. I have pressure and every time I try to touch my toes it hurts. I be forgetting to stretch every time. Now I do it first, whenever I go outside.

Grandma Velez

I was really close to my mom's mom. I was with her when she passed. There was an argument with my dad and mom about my bike. I broke it and didn't tell no one. My dad said, "Let's go bike riding," and I said that I had a flat. I kept saying that for a few days, and he kept telling me to fix it. I had bent the rim, and finally he looked at it. He yelled at me for lying to him.

I know I was wrong. But my mom took my side. My grandma told me to come to bed to calm the argument. She was eating some soup, finished, and we went to my room that I shared with her. She brushed her teeth and came into the room. Then she prayed and laid down next to me to make me feel better. Then she just sat up and suddenly laid on her stomach, which she never ever did. So I looked at her, and this white stuff came from her mouth. I knew she passed away. She always listened to what I had to say, gave me advice, and protected me. Now she was gone.

A Day for Each Other

This is the first Father's Day that my dad and I will be alone. I'm not sure what we're going to do. I'm just going to live it. I'm just going to be with my dad and go do something. Get out of the house. But not the movies, 'cause in the movies you don't talk, you just watch and can think about other things. Something has to be going on. Maybe play basketball together or hang out with somebody. We have to leave the house—it's more exciting to try new stuff, and you already know what you're going to do in the house. It's also easier not to be around the memories.

Moving
Away
from Pain

My dad and I are hoping to move, to try something new. I want to move far, but my dad wants to stay close. Maybe we'll go to Castle Hill so my dad could be close to his mom. My dad worries about his mom. And if we're nearby, she could still cook for us.

I think we could use something new after everything that happened in that apartment. It would be like a different environment, so we could think about different things. Take the good thoughts and leave the bad.

Keeping
Secrets

My dad doesn't keep secrets from me 'cause he loves me
too much. He doesn't keep secrets from me 'cause he
doesn't want me to keep secrets from him. Sacrificing the
truth is not always good. He tells me everything and
wants me to do the same. Even if it's something bad, he
just wants me to tell him the truth, so I won't have to be
going through something even longer. The truth makes
things end sooner—even bad things, 'cause eventually it
comes out. So it's better to deal with it. I don't always do
it, even though I know my dad is right.

Un-Social Worker

I've got to get on my father's case. I don't mean his back,
I mean on his case for, like, Medicaid and all that. I'm
under my mom's name, not my dad's name, 'cause they
were never married. So I got to go under my dad's name
so I can get covered.

It's hard 'cause it's taking some time, 'cause the
social worker don't have the time to send in all the
papers and all that. The social worker has too many people to take care of, so it's taking months. If it takes this
long, the social worker must have a lot to do.

I met the social worker once, and he was okay, but
I don't really remember him much. My mom told me

about him. She said he always takes forever to do anything. Plus, he screamed at her. He said something about her personal business, about her and my father being together. He made her cry 'cause he was criticizing her. I know now what she meant about taking too long, 'cause now I'm waiting.

Santeria

After my grandmother died, I saw her shadow. She could visit 'cause she was into Santeria. She used to always go to the Botanica. It's a store that has candles, statues, and stuff like that. She believed in using these things. She would light the candles in the house for different reasons, but only for good things. If someone passed away, she would light a candle for them, or for the santo statue as an offering. If someone was sick, she would smoke the house to get rid of the bad spirits. She used to put these ingredients in a pan, burn them, and smoke would come out. She would take the pot and go around the house with it to smoke the house.

I used to see things like she did. I saw my grandmother's mom, who I never met. I wouldn't be thinking about anything and I saw a ghost walking at me and disappear. I saw things walking around like spirits. But only me and my grandmother could see these things. She would use the smoke to get rid of them. She only used Santeria to protect the family.

Then, after she passed, I heard my grandmother's slippers and saw her shadow on the wall. I told her I didn't want to see the visions anymore 'cause they were scary. And she took them with her, so I never saw the spirits again.

Responsibility

The biggest responsibility I had was taking care of my mother. My dad told me I had to watch over my mom 'cause she was sick. I thought I could do it, mainly 'cause I wanted to do it. I wanted to help her. Sometimes I felt it was too much, 'cause she was so sick, but I wanted to do it, so I just did it.

When you have responsibility to do something, people have confidence in you doing the job. They know that you're able to do it. If you can't, you should tell them rather than let it go. It's good to have responsibility, 'cause it's a lot of trust. It's 'cause they trust you that they give you responsibility. I try to be responsible, and if someone tells me to do something, I try to do it.

I have to be responsible to my father and not make him worry about things. So I do what I have to do. But it doesn't always happen, so he gets mad. I know he's right, so it makes it easier to listen to him even when I don't want to. Sometimes he takes it to the extreme, but only when I let the same thing go over and over again.

Now I have responsibility for myself—to do what's

best for me. Like going to school: it's good for me. I have to look at school differently, so I'm going to change schools to be what I want. I also want to be a better basketball player, so that's another responsibility.

First Time for Everything

This girl from upstairs asked me to take her to her prom. I wore my navy blue jacket and pants, with a turtleneck and some gold chains and my shoes. She had on, like, this white dress and high heels. She's just a little shorter than me. She has nice hair, it's short and brown. She's pretty.

Someone drove us to White Plains to the Harbor Restaurant. As you walked in, there was a bar, but that was for the older guys. Straight through, there was a room with chairs and a DJ. It was nice, decorated and all.

There was a lot of girls, and I was flirting a lot. My date didn't mind, 'cause when the girls asked if I was her boyfriend, she said no. She didn't want to dance much 'cause of her high heels. So when the other girls asked me to dance, she told me to go dance.

I didn't know everybody, but they all seemed to like me. They played music—old and new, Spanish and Latin, salsa and rap. I also danced slow with a lot of girls. Not all the guys there knew how to dance in different styles, but I had taught myself. I got busy dancing. I danced with five girls at one time. They surrounded me dancing a reggae song. They were all up on me—bumping legs on me, grinding till they sandwiched me. They were dancing every way, surrounding me, yelling, "We got him now!" I didn't even taste the buffet food; I had a headache from dancing!

There was a girl there. Her name was Veronica.* She's very tall with black hair and a nice smile. She was easy to talk to, so I got her number. I don't know where we'll go, but I'm going to ask her out.

*I changed her name so she wouldn't be embarrassed.

Dad's Job

Sometimes I'll be thinking about things but not say anything about it. Even if I get in trouble, I just wait till I get caught. I know it's bad 'cause I get tense and all that. I worry about what will happen, 'cause sooner or later it comes out. I just wait to get caught, so I get all anxious. The best thing to do is not go wrong in the first place, but if you do, you should tell someone. I know that that's right, but I don't always do it.

Some things I don't like to talk about with my dad. Like girls. I told him about that girl Veronica. He said, "Forget about her, 'cause she wasn't in your life until last night." He doesn't want girls to take up my time. He thinks I should focus on other things, like school. He's worried that she'll influence me. He worries about kids my age having sex, babies, and abortions. I know that it's bad to be having sex at this age, 'cause it stops you from doing school and stuff, but I wouldn't let being with a girl stop me from doing what I got to be doing. So I disagree with him 'cause I want to have a girl.

My dad says that there are other things in my life, like school, basketball, writing, and exploring stuff, but today he asked me to bring Veronica over so he could meet her. You know, to see how she is. I think he changed his mind, 'cause at first he said he didn't want me to have a girlfriend till I was nineteen. He said, "It's not that. I want you to keep focus." He wants me to do well, but he knows there are other things in life.

Learning
Without a Cause

Kids don't always think they will use what they learn in school. Like they think that what they learn from first to eighth is used, 'cause it's adding, subtracting, and multiplying. But they think that from ninth to twelfth they won't use it, 'cause it's questions like $y = x$ and algebra. They say they won't have use for that in life. They get bored and say they're not going to use it on a job, so it's a waste of time. It's true that they don't know what kind of job they will eventually have, but they don't know of any type of job that uses geometry. It's hard for them to see that they'll need it unless they want to be a scientist. It seems like teachers just want to see if you can learn something.

The same is true for science. They think you need it if you want to make things like a light bulb or discover stuff. To kids, science is for technology, but it's not real. So why should they learn it? This goes for English, too, where you have to read stories. If what you're reading is not true, like a kid getting lost in the woods, why should you read it? It didn't happen! But if you can learn something real, you're more interested in it. Some kids see reading stories as entertaining, but others aren't interested. Kids are interested in learning about certain things. They want to know about facts or things they can relate to. This makes more sense in their lives than made-up stories or myths.

Kids call history, "His Story." They feel that yesterday was history and tomorrow is a mystery. They are worried about the future. They want to know what's *going to* happen, not what *already* happened. They say it's His Story, not my story. They say, "That's what happened to other people, but why worry about them? Yeah, they had wars and everything, but it's the past. We're not going through it now, so let's worry about the future."

I feel there are certain subjects that are not for me, like algebra. But I guess it's good to know, 'cause as you get older, you might change and not know now what you'll need. So I guess it's good to learn everything you can now, but it would be better if kids could be told what it's all for.

It's Mandatory

All kids at some time in the ninth, tenth, or eleventh grade have to take the RCT test until they pass it. It's a test you have to take before you graduate high school. It was easy for me. It was Math and the questions were easy. I spoke to my math teacher about it. She had given us a pretest to get ready. The one she gave us was real easy, so I asked her, "It's going to be similar, right?" And she said yes. I thought it was seventh-grade work. So then my teacher told me that next year the Board of Education is going to change it and it won't be this easy.

The first two pages of the test were crazy easy. Adding, division, and subtracting was easy. After that, they got into $3y = x$. They also give you English and Reading, but I had passed them already.

The test is a review to make sure that if you're graduated from the seventh and eigth grade, it wasn't 'cause they just passed you through. It shows that you know the work and you're ready. It's good. This way they don't just throw you to the world when you're not ready for it. Then all that school would be a waste of time.

School is supposed to help you and not make you feel dumb. If you're not ready, you know you have to work on it. If you are ready, the test makes you feel better. But you can't help but feel it's a test just to see what you learned. So it's, like, for the school, not you.

Giving Math a Different Perspective

Math can be fun, but when it gets to the extreme, it's kind of boring. It's like stacks—like trying to build with bricks. You need one thing to know about the brick that goes on top of it, and if you miss that first brick, you are not going to know how to do what's next. There are always stages you have to go through. You have to know this stage to get to the next stage. You have to learn both of those stages to get to the third stage. If you miss or don't understand one stage, the whole thing messes up and collapses on you. Now that I been thinking about this, I feel that this may be true for everything you learn.

When You Read What Interests You

This year, English has been my favorite subject, 'cause we're into reading stories. We would read each story and answer questions about what happened. The questions would ask what a certain character did or said. It was fun, and knowing you had to answer the questions made you read the story more carefully. There were a lot of stories.

The one I remember most was called "The Most Dangerous Game." It was exciting, and you couldn't help but get into it. This guy is on this island. He had been knocked out, and when he woke up he was walking around in the dark. When you're reading it in the beginning and it says "The Most Dangerous Game," you wonder why it's called that. Then you start getting into it and you say, "Oh, yeah, that explains the title." This character is afraid of the other people he saw on the island. He wanted to know more about them but needed their help 'cause his boat had crashed. So he didn't know what to do. Then the story goes on for three more pages, and you realize this guy's getting hunted. It's exciting the way he tries to survive, what he is doing, the time he almost gets caught, and just when you think he's going to get caught, there's three other pages where he's escaping and getting hunted again.

I felt like I was there and didn't know what would happen next. The words the author used and the detail are great. Like when he wrote that the guy was running through the woods and he was so tired he had to stop, but couldn't breathe hard, 'cause the people chasing him would hear. I was thinking to myself that would be hard to do and everything and, if I was that guy, I would do the same. I like when we talk about it after we read it. It makes the exciting parts happen again.

Teacher
Knows What's Up

Hygiene class teaches you about a lot of different things, so you don't get bored like with one subject. You get to learn about your body, sex education, drugs, and peer pressure. It's about a lot of issues you go through. So you learn about a little bit of everything.

The lady who teaches the class is open to all our questions and answers whatever we ask. Some kids play dumb, so they ask questions for a joke. They do this to be funny to the other kids and be clever, and to make the teacher look silly. She knows the deal. She smiles and says, "Stop playing." She's a good teacher. She knows a lot of stuff and she knows us.

Knowing
When

To have a relationship with a female, I think you should be sixteen or seventeen. I know I'm only fifteen, but I'm going to be sixteen. I don't necessarily want to be in, like, a "relationship," but I want to go out with girls. I feel like I'm old enough 'cause I know about a lot of things. It's a good age.

You should be a little more mature and be able to make decisions. To do that, you should know what's right and what's wrong, what you should do and what you shouldn't. So I think it's a good age to know what's going on with your life, and know when to say no to anything you shouldn't do. Like about having sex, hanging out, or using drugs. With the right person, you can avoid those problems and say, "Let's stay home and do something else." You can cut out the extra activity. You know how it is and what you want. When you know a little more about yourself, you can know what it is to be with someone else.

Veronica

I visited my old school to see Veronica, the girl I met at the prom. I told the school guards I came to see my old teachers, but I really wanted to see her. I was looking for her but didn't see her until just before I left. She was having lunch, but I couldn't talk to her or nothing 'cause I wasn't allowed in the cafeteria. So I just saw her. I want to call her, but she can't have phone calls from boys. I can't see her, 'cause her mom and dad are strict. No boys at all. I don't know what I'm going to do. I have to figure it out.

My friend Thom has been teaching me photography. He showed me once how to use a really good camera. Then I just got camera-happy and was taking pictures of everything. I would take pictures looking for action or just the right pose. It's exciting to plan and catch it.

Snapping with a View

I'm still learning about the lighting. I don't have it down pat. Before you take a picture in an area, you have to put the light meter up and look to see if it goes to a certain number. You have to put the camera to the same number. Then, when you take a picture, it will look better, 'cause the light will make it clearer.

Taking basketball pictures is really exciting—taking snaps in action. Plus, I like the sport, so it's like I'm taking pictures for <u>Sports</u> <u>Illustrated</u> or something. There's a difference when you take pictures of a place, 'cause there's no action to catch. Like when you snap and the basketball just left the guy's fingertips and he puts his hand on his face, it's like you froze a moment. But with a place it has to be interesting on its own. If it looks good to me, I'm going to take it, 'cause it means something to me and to other people, too.

Photography is still new and I'm still learning about it. I have to do it more to see if it's something I'll always do.

Not Going My Way

I want to go out with Veronica, but now the girl that took me to her prom likes me—a lot! She lives upstairs, and at first it didn't seem like she liked me. Now it's like she's in love with me. My dad and I are always at it, 'cause he don't want me to have a girl at all, but this girl keeps at it. I know if I asked her out, she would definitely say yes, 'cause she calls me all the time. The problem is, the only way I can find out about Veronica is by talking to this other girl. She calls me every day and would talk for hours. With her, one phone call is enough.

So I try to play her, to find out about Veronica. I asked this other girl, "Did anyone at the prom talk about me?" She said yeah, this person, this girl, and this girl. So I gave her the name of another girl, who is really ugly. She knows I would never ask her out and she says, "Oh, yeah," and she tells me what was said. Then I went through all her friends till I got to Veronica. I told her I liked two girls: her and Veronica. She said, "Oh."

Next, she told me that every day they kept asking her if I was her boyfriend and hassling her. So I said, "If it's so bad, just say yes." The next day in school, she told everyone. But I don't want Veronica to hear that there is another girl. I know I was, like, leading her on. I like her as a friend, but I want to go out with Veronica. Now I got this other girl saying I'm her boyfriend. Things aren't working the way I had planned.

Losing Friends

I never had a friend die, but I lost a lot of kids 'cause they got into something I was not interested in. Or they're not interested in the things I do, 'cause it doesn't go to their level. They're into, like, more daring things. They criticize me, saying I'm just living an everyday life, that I have to be in at a certain time, I'm not doing drugs, I can't go to parties, or I'm not having sex.

We don't have anything in common. I don't want to do what they do, and they don't want to do what I do. They feel that my life is not exciting enough, while I feel theirs is just unnecessary. Like, if they're using drugs, having sex, or hanging out. I just want to have fun and not be hanging out with the wrong crowd.

I just lost friendships 'cause I felt they would take me someplace I didn't want to go. Something is going to happen bad if you hang out, 'cause even if you don't want to do the things they do, if you continue to hang out with them, eventually you will do something serious. It will add up and get worse.

I miss them for the things we used to do, like playing ball and joking around. But that was when we were young. Now I'm just trying to grow out of it, but they're still doing the same things. I want to move on, but it's lonely.

Making the Right Deci

I think kids are scared about sex 'cause they're just kids. They're scared of death or catching the disease. So they're going to use a condom. But if they don't have it and it's right there and then and they been going out with the person, they won't use protection.

If there is a condom in another room or nearby, they probably would get it, 'cause it's just there. It also depends on where they're having sex. If they're in a house and their parents aren't there, it's more likely they'll use a condom. But if they're having sex in the hall, on a roof, or someplace outside, they might not have one with them. So there's a good chance that kids will use condoms if they have one. If not, they won't.

I know this, 'cause kids are having babies and abortions like crazy. So, if this is happening, I know kids are not using condoms. They feel they know their boyfriend or girlfriend: they're always with them and they're going out. They think they would know if they were with other people who are sick. So they trust each other. But someone doesn't always know if they have it.

The other thing is, not every kid knows how to use a condom perfectly. I know, 'cause my Dad had taught me how to use it exactly, even though he doesn't want me to date girls. But most kids' parents that I know don't teach their kids. They don't want their kids to have sex at a young age. The parents say, "You're not having sex, period.

I'm not teaching you, 'cause you're not having sex and that's that. No sex until you're older." So they feel they don't have to teach kids, 'cause they think then they won't have sex. They'll tell the girls, "Don't be fresh. Don't let no guys touch you or influence you or nothing." They tell the boys that if they get some girl pregnant, their life is ruined.

You can tell kids not to have sex. I don't think that's bad. But actually stopping them from having sex, it's just the kids' decision. And there are a lot of other influences. I think girls give sex more thought, but the boys act it out more.

93
• • •

Talk Is Cheap

I think to be having sex, you should be an age not in your teens. Not at all. In grades from one to twelve, you're not ready. There are, like, five different stages in your life: Preteen, teen, young adult, adult and older. I feel that before you have sex, you should know what you want to do with your life. At least do something with your life. To really explain it, it's better if you have something good going for your life before you have sex, 'cause there's always a chance you could have a kid.

If you have a life, and you're in your twenties, you

know what's going to be better for yourself and your partner and anybody else that may be involved. At least, you should have your own apartment and job. You shouldn't be doing it in somebody else's house. You should know how to live on your own and know a little about life. When you're ready to have sex is when you're older, in your twenties. It's an adult thing, so you should be an adult.

I know this is not always realistic, 'cause kids ain't waiting that long. It's ridiculous to think they would. Today, if you're a virgin at sixteen, they ask what's wrong with you. The average kid I know is having sex at thirteen, 'cause it's when you first become a teen and you think you know it all already. The kids say, "I'm a teenager. I'm cool. I know what I'm doing." Kids pressure each other to have sex.

At this age, girls are easily influenced. If a boy hangs around with them and gives them jewelry and everything, and their mother allows them to go out, they feel it's okay because they are all grown up. The girl feels she is really falling in love and it will be forever. She doesn't realize she's not grown up, especially when her friends push her to go out. It's easier then for her to make the decision to have sex, because she wants people to think of her as grown-up.

The boys say, "Hey, I'm having sex. I'm a man." To be a virgin, they think, makes them not be a man. If you're going out with someone, kids feel you have to be having sex with them. They feel that if you are going out with someone and not having sex, you're a punk. They have to prove it to themselves and their friends.

Scandals

When somebody famous, like a sports figure or singing star, gets into trouble, kids take it a lot of ways. If it's someone they don't like, they say, "See, I told you." They say they knew the person wasn't perfect or that they knew they were hiding something. The point is that no one is perfect, but when the kids see it, it's a big deal.

But when it's someone the kids like and know is talented, they snap on them anyway, 'cause in reality these people aren't doing anything for the kids.

Sometimes it's disappointing. Like with Michael Jackson, it was hard to hear bad things about him 'cause of all the things he was doing for kids, like the charity to save kids from starving. Everyone was looking at him as a role model. The next thing you know, this kid said those things about him. It was bad, 'cause someone like Michael Jackson doesn't have to do charity, give food to people and all that, but he's doing it from his heart. So when he got caught, even though we don't know if it was really true, it was disappointing. He was not only a singer. He was someone who was helping out.

So the kids feel betrayed. A lot of kids don't even know if they're good.

I learned
hat there are
ard times to be
ad. I felt good at
ne moment and
hen, for a long
hile, I felt bad.
    It was like
 nightmare
hat I couldn'
ake up from.
t happened
o quickly,
ike a snap.
ut I see that
f you just co
inue your lif
t will get
etter.
f you think
ou're facing
he hardest
bstacle you
o face, just
oing. It's part
f life.

Don't Shoot! It's Just a Camera

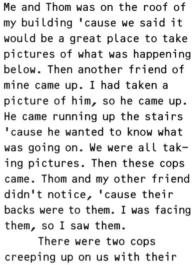

Me and Thom was on the roof of my building 'cause we said it would be a great place to take pictures of what was happening below. Then another friend of mine came up. I had taken a picture of him, so he came up. He came running up the stairs 'cause he wanted to know what was going on. We were all taking pictures. Then these cops came. Thom and my other friend didn't notice, 'cause their backs were to them. I was facing them, so I saw them.

There were two cops creeping up on us with their guns out, pointing at us. The cops said, "What are you doing up here? You know you're not supposed to be up here." So Thom quickly gave them an explanation of why we were up there taking pictures. The cops said we could take more pictures while they were up there with us. So I decided to take a picture of them. The cops stayed up there with us for a while.

I know why the cops came. A lot of people go to the roof to shoot guns or do drugs. So

97
...

the cops don't want people on the roof, to avoid accidents or bad things like that. I know it's true, 'cause I heard shots from the roof. I've gotten woken up with the gunshots. I don't always know where it's coming from. It was scary for a bit, but I understand why the cops came.

We finished and went down the stairs but the cops stayed. They were on the roof, 'cause they can see all the roofs from there.

Room for Improvement

I should be a better person. I should feel better about myself. I want to feel comfortable with who I am and what I'm doing. You know, comfortable with my inner self, knowing what I'm doing is right. A real positive change would be if I could depend more on myself to put on the limits. I think about, if I do certain things, I might get in trouble, but I still do them. I want to be able to stop myself.

Now I do good things and bad things, but I want to get to the point in my life where I just do good things.

By taking every chance I get and being able to stop myself from doing what's wrong, I can stop depending on my father. I'm glad that my father says things like "Don't do drugs. Don't hang out." I'm glad he don't okay it. If he okayed the bad things, I would probably like him more at the time, but later I would hate him for letting me do all the wrong things.

There will be a time when I'm old enough or ready to set limits for myself, like when I'm able to vote and can pay my rent. I should be able to do it then: it will be my decision. I'll be able to do what I want, so I'll have to be *sure* it's right.

Professor Jordan

My favorite dream had me meeting every famous basketball player. I was in school, and the players were teaching us basketball. In every class I went to that day, there was a famous player instead of the teacher. They then autographed my basketball cards so they were worth more. I guess this is something I wish would happen. I don't know what I would say if it really happened other than "Teach me." They could show me better moves, and I could play like them. To get it direct from the players, that's a dream.

Trash
Talking

In the game of basketball, trash talking is part of the deal. While you're playing, people be saying they're better than you, that you can't play, or just insult you. It puts people on the spot. Like, I'm playing, and this guy playing defense on me is saying, "You're not going to score nothing. I'm going to score more than you. Let me get the ball." So when someone's trash talking, you have to prove yourself to him, but mostly to yourself. No matter what they say, you can't believe them.

When I'm feeling good about myself, trash talking is not a problem. But if I start a game and miss my first five shots, I feel that's how I'm going to play the whole game. If I make the first five shots, I have more confidence. I'm ready for trash talking. It depends on how I start. If it's a great start, that's how I'm going to finish it. If I have a bad start, that's how I'm going to finish.

I think trash talking can also give you confidence, but my dad doesn't like it when I do it. But I think it works. Like, I would say, "You can't score on me." You try to get them out of their game. You get them so mad, they're not into the game, they're into you. So you take them out of the game and put yourself in the game more.

Making Up
for Lost Time

'Cause of everything that was going on with my mom, I would stay home from school just to be with her and my dad. When I got back, I had to catch up, 'cause I missed the beginning of every subject. I don't think I lost a year, but I did lose a lot of work. I have to go to summer school for everything they offer.

I have to do this to be ready for a new school. In a way, I like the idea of a new school. It's exciting, 'cause I don't know anything about it. It's like a suspenseful mystery, except it will be fun. People will be thinking, "Who's this kid?" and I can show who I am now. They will know me only for who I am now. I want them to think I'm bright, funny, and easy to get along with. In the beginning, I'll be myself, nice. I'll be able to start fresh. It will be hard, but I feel like a young adult now and that's how I want people to know me.

Competition

Competition can prove that you are better than other people at doing the things you like to do. It gives you pressure, but I like it, 'cause if you can do a good job under pressure, you really succeed. Of course, if you don't come out on top, it's messed up and you still have to get yourself ready for the next competition.

Competition is really what you think it is. It could be with schoolwork, having friends, or even what kind of clothes you wear. Whatever it is, you have to deal with it the right way. You have to give it, like, a real perspective. Competition makes some people choke, but for others it makes them do their very best. I think it makes me play basketball better. But when you get competitive about everything, you miss the fun of living.

Veronica: The Master Plan

I finally told the girl upstairs (from the prom thing) that I really like Veronica. I wrote a note in her yearbook to Veronica, since I still cannot get to talk to Veronica directly. The other girl said it would be all right and even said she would talk to Veronica for me.

So I wrote in the yearbook, "Veronica, Hi! I'm sorry we couldn't get to know each other better. I hope we still could." Then I got a great idea. I thought it would be nice to invite her to a youth luncheon that I was asked to speak at. I'm going to invite her parents, too, since they're strict and won't let her go out or talk to me. But if they see me speak at the youth group they may say, "Hey, this kid is pretty good!" I'll just have to wait.

Bad Thoughts

Suicide is always on somebody's mind, people thinking that "I should kill myself and everything would stop"—but it's not that way. When all these bad things were happening to me, I thought about it. Not in the action way, but I thought about it. Then I just pushed it out of my mind. I didn't allow myself to think about it. You can't dwell on it.

It was hard to do that, but I thought, "It isn't right." I know suicide is wrong, 'cause if I die, even more people would suffer. Like my family and friends. I know now what it's like to lose someone you love.

I think that people who commit suicide must be confused. They can't express themselves and feel they are going through more things then anybody else and are all alone. So they commit suicide 'cause they think things won't change. They see it as an escape. I don't see it that way. I know what all those feelings are like, but suicide is not an escape. Your friends and family don't get to escape! And I have learned that even the most horrible things change.

Mother's Day

On Mother's Day, I went to St. Patrick's
Cathedral to light a candle for my mother.
She had just passed, and it was good to
remember her in this beautiful church. I
was amazed by the paintings, the statues,
and the stained glass. I thought that the
different ways these things were done was
interesting. It was nice 'cause the
church was so big and filled with so many
beautiful things. Lighting a candle for
my mom at this particular church made me
feel good. I prayed and it was like I was
with her, in the only way I can be now.

Surprised to Fight,
But I Knew
the Outcome

This kid Alex* and I had a fight. It was like a draw. So this other kid named Eric* decided he didn't like me. I don't know why. He just felt he could beat me and that's all. I used to tell him he couldn't, but then he saw me fight Alex and got all macho.

I didn't know Eric was planning to fight me. The next day, when I walked out of Gym, I saw everyone just standing around. I said to myself, "Wow, it's a big crowd. There's going to be a good fight." I wanted to make sure I got to the front row and all that. I didn't know that I would have to be in the front row 'cause I was the main event.

So I was just walking through. The next thing I know, I'm walking into it. I was wondering why people were not shoving me out of the way so they can see the fight—they were just letting me go by. Then I see *I'm* in the fight. I had to put on a little show. Eric was there and he had some excuse that I took his social studies homework. It wasn't true, but he just needed any excuse to fight me.

*I changed their names.

We put down our book bags and started fighting. I was just knocking him out. I kept punching him until he was on the floor. Just knocking him out, knocking him out. Finally, it got broken up and we went to class. His face was all messed up, 'cause I used to wrestle a lot, so I was more powerful than him.

I didn't want to fight him, but I had to. He's the one that threw the first punch, and there was a lot of kids there. If I would have walked away, I would have had more fights, 'cause everybody would have picked on me. He set it up so I had to fight him. It was embarrassing to him, 'cause he's the one that wanted to fight and he lost, and he lost—badly. I feel that if you don't start a fight, you always win, 'cause you have less to lose.

Fighting Without a Cause

I used to fight a lot 'cause I liked to fight. I don't know why. I didn't even think about it. I just wanted to fight 'cause I didn't have anything better to do. I didn't have an agenda. I never thought I should play basketball or I should do anything. I didn't know what to do outside, so I said I'll just fight. Fighting became the activity.

I didn't even have a reason to fight with the people I did. It was just to fight. I made up the reason. I just got fight happy. It made me pumped. I wanted the other kids to be scared of me, and it worked. Someone just comes outside and looks at you and asks if you're okay. Then I would fight them. I used to get dressed up just to fight. Put sweats on, my sneakers, be all loose and ready.

I used to have kids I made a "regular." I'd pick some kid, and every time I saw them outside, I would fight them. Like if I'd had an argument with the kid before, he'd become a regular. It was like I was confused. I didn't know what to do with myself or who to be. It was something I did, but now I don't know why.

Mistakes Happen

I got suspended from school for one day over breaking the locks with my friend. They called my house and said that now I am suspended. I didn't think it was a big deal. What I think should have happened is they should have made me fix it. But they fixed it already. One day isn't a real punishment. It doesn't change things, and most kids who get in trouble don't want to be in school in the first place.

I told the school dean I was sorry. And I really felt it. I wasn't sorry for getting caught, I was sorry for what I did and had no real reason to do it. It was stupid. I, like, slipped back.

I'm Not Perfect

No one's perfect. I know this saying is true, but you can try to be. Everybody's going to make mistakes in their life. That's how you learn. If you don't make mistakes, how else would you learn? But a bad mistake can hit you real hard. You say to yourself, "I made a mistake and everything happened."

It's good to make your mistakes early in life, so they don't become big mistakes when you're older. I know the mistakes I made—fighting, breaking things in school, and doing dumb daring things. One time on a dare from a friend, I put a smoke bomb in this car muffler. I knew it wouldn't blow up or nothing, just smoke. So I put it there, and the owner of the car was right there. He grabbed me, picked me up, shook me, and threw me on the floor in front of everyone. I thought the smoke bomb would be a big joke, but the joke was on me.

Going
Through
Bad Times

When I thought about how my mom was suffering in the hospital, I got depressed. I know I was depressed 'cause I was scared, and worried and I couldn't think about other things. I tried to keep myself busy, but I still couldn't stop thinking about it. I knew what was going to happen to my mom. That's why it was so extreme. I knew she had to pass away.

It was a long time that she was sick, so in a way I was ready. If she had just died, it might have been harder. But if you see someone sick for months and months and months, you are already coping with it. You get to understand and think about the consequences. But sometimes, even knowing what will happen and having dealt with it for a long time, you still get depressed.

Bring in the Morning

Bring in the Morning was a show about kids who come from, like, my neighborhood. This was the first time I went to a real theater for a show. It was exciting, 'cause there was music with a beat, dancing I like, and singing. I thought the songs were good 'cause they were positive about the problems you go through every day in your heart.

I imagined myself on stage with them. I thought I couldn't do it the way they were 'cause I don't have a voice. I could do the acting part and the dancing part, but that's as far as it goes. I think I'd like to be a performer, and seeing people who come from my neighborhood able to be on stage made me feel like I could. It was a real thing, especially since they were young, even though a lot of them were in their twenties.

I related to the performers. The set was nice, with the smoke, the paintings, and the lights. I liked the projections they used in back. They reminded me of where I live. It was better then television, 'cause with television, you just be watching. In the theater you feel it. You're more into it. You get the energy.

The Big Question

I was invited to speak at a breakfast for New York City schools' chancellor, Ramon Cortines, 'cause one of the subjects I was writing for this book was about being a student in this city. I was seated next to Mr. Cortines, and he asked me to call him Ray. He likes to be called Ray: it's, like, less formal. He and I was talking and laughing. He's a friendly type.

I was told to ask him a question when he got up to talk with the audience and the press. I had a question that had been on my mind. I told him the question before he spoke, so it could be more easy for him to talk about. This way his answer could be thought out. I didn't want to put him on the spot, either. I said to him, "This is the question I'm going to ask you later on." He said, "Thank you. At least someone's looking out for me."

When Ray got up to speak, I asked my question: "One of the big problems in schools is the kids' attitudes, which is why they don't attend. Many kids don't understand what certain subjects have to do with their lives. Would it be possible to change things and include in the curriculum advice, so that when you are in english, math, and science classes, the teachers explain how the kids will use what they learn in getting a job and in their lives?"

His answer was that he would like to be able to do what I asked, and I think that he really would like to do it. But he made it sound like it would be hard. He said he would need the right people and he couldn't really tell me how it would work.

But I wonder why it would be so hard. Couldn't you just make it the teachers' business to do it? It should be part of their job when they're teaching class. They have to give explanations. They have to teach certain steps so kids can learn something. Like, when they develop the curriculum, couldn't teachers include an explanation of how to use what they teach? It's still a question for me.

Veronica: The Plan Goes On

I called Veronica's parents to invite them all to the breakfast for Board of Education chancellor Cortines. Her mom answered and said that they couldn't make it, 'cause her son was getting an operation that day. I was able to meet Veronica's father. He said that the family would also like to meet me. Veronica is also going to work around my area with her father, so I can have lunch with her. At lunchtime, I'll stop by and bring some treats. Her parents will let me see her. It looks like my plan worked.

Trying Again

I'm scared to float. If I try, when I start sinking, I just jump right back up. I think I'm going to go down and that water's going to go up my nose. I hate that. But I'm going to do it with goggles and try again. I can swim, but I'm too tense to float. I'm always thinking that I'm going down. But I'll keep trying, 'cause I wonder how it feels to float.

and Again

Free
for
Now

In the summer, you're free. Free from school and heavy clothes. Summer is for enjoyment. I think of summer as my time or anybody's time. Usually for me, I use my time for basketball. I think summertime is best for sports. When I play in the summer, I play the best. All day, every day. More kids are out, and more is happening.

It's like Sunday. You don't have to worry about waking up. You don't have to wait for the weekend to play all day. It just dawns on me, "Wow, I don't have to get up on Monday and I can play all day." All of a sudden I'll be real happy, 'cause there is nothing I have to do. I'm just all over happiness.

Paid Protection

There's a security guard at my school who sells Cool Waters Cologne to the kids. Every day, he sells Cool Waters, Midnight, or different types of cologne for four dollars a bottle. I think, 'cause it's high school, that the kids are old enough to buy it if they want. Since he brings it every day, he should be making some business. He has these three-inch bottles in his pockets. It's like cologne from the stores.

I say to the security guard, "Let me see the Cool Waters." He lets me see it, 'cause he thinks I'm going to buy it. I dab a little bit on and just give it back to him. He says, "You always do that to me. Putting on my stuff and don't buy it and walk away." But he keeps giving it to me, 'cause he wants the money and thinks maybe I'll really buy it this time. The kids are friendly with him and all the security guards. I tease them 'cause they have to wear polyester uniforms. In the summertime they be all hot.

All the security guards are cool. They all got their certain way, except for Ice. He's the only one the kids think is uncool, 'cause he busts them if they're cutting. A lot of the kids think it's uncool, 'cause most of the guards won't bust you. But he's doing his job. They all should be doing what he does. They do protect the kids, but they don't push it.

The other guards watch the entrance, and kids say, "Let me out to the store and I'll be right back." They let them go, and sometimes the guard with the cologne would tell the kids to buy him something. So the kids would, like, have to buy him a soda or ice cream, depending on what he asked for. I think that Ice is really doing the best job. That's why the kids don't like him.

Family Matters

Close to where I live is my father's sister, Aunt Luz, and his brother, Uncle Ruben. My Aunt Luz's oldest son is Andy. He is eighteen. He used to go to the cadets and liked it a lot, but he likes girls a lot, too. He would always get into trouble 'cause of it. He is doing okay, messing up a little. He just always talking about girls. Then he had a kid, but he left and went to Florida to work with his dad. We used to have fun talking about girls and a lot of other things. We used to always snap on each other. I miss that.

Andy has two younger brothers and a younger sister, and I'm close to all of them. One boy, Jose, is ten. The other, Canno, is seven. The girl, Lisa, is sixteen. She is smart in school and has boyfriends. Unlike my dad, her parents let her date. When I go over there, there are more girls to meet, 'cause Lisa's friends from school are there. It's fun.

Aunt Luz is always cooking, like, chicken, rice, and pork chops. It's the regular food I like. I play Sega Genesis with the boys. It's like a warm place to go. Right next door is my Uncle Ruben and his wife and two-year-old daughter. I like to play with their daughter. She reminds me of how my little sister was.

There's a park nearby to play basketball, and I made a lot of friends in just under a week 'cause I know about playing basketball so well. The kids say, "Pick him, pick him—he knows how to play."

My mother's family lives far away, so I don't see them. Still it's great, 'cause I have, like, two other families that I can be part of.

The Big One!

One birthday I had, Mom was joking around and threw cake in my face. She cut a piece and squashed it in my face. I did it right back. She screamed not to do it hard.

But the most memorable birthday was when she threw a big party for me. She paid for a DJ 'cause it was my first teen birthday. I was thirteen. It was a big party with dancing. My mom always liked to dance.

There were a lot of people, about fifty. There was food and a big cake. We didn't eat the cake that day, 'cause people would have dogged it. They would have just ate it quick, and I wouldn't have gotten a piece. We put it away for the next day and had another party for just us.

Good Times

My mom would always want me to talk with her, or do something with her, or teach her a new dance step. She would say, "Teach me the new steps they have." She was always interested in me. She would always tell me that she wouldn't want me with an ugly girl, 'cause I was so handsome. If she was cooking, she would say, "Gil come over here, I want you to be over here so we can talk." We would talk, talk, talk.

And we'd kid around, like me scaring her with a fake mouse. I would say to her, "Did you hear that?" She would say, "What?" I'd say "There's a mouse in the kitchen. I'll go check it out." And I would leave and grab my fake mouse by the tail then comeback and shake it, and she'd scream. And then I would laugh. She would be mad—not real mad, but laughing mad. She knows she can't get even, 'cause I would always think of something else.

I went to California with my mom when I was younger. I remember she was scared of the rides, so when we went to Disneyland she just watched. I tried to convince her, but she wouldn't. We had fun at Universal Studios and Knott's Berry Farm. She would go on tours and look at the rides, but never get on. I have pictures and memories of Mom.

The Scariest Part of Being an Adult

The scariest part of being an adult to me is making your own decisions. The real scary part is knowing if your decisions are right. The right decision is better for you in the long run, but the wrong decision will mess you up along the way. If you make the decision to do nothing, it's not good. If you can take advantage of an opportunity, you should. You can really benefit yourself. The decision part makes it scary. You need to think it out. Think how the decision will feel in the long run, not just now, 'cause your decision will have a future, too.

Why or Why Not Me?

Sometimes I wonder why things happen to me. Not only the bad things, but the good things, too. If something good is happening, I say someone is watching over me. But I worry. If so many good things happen to me as a kid, something drastic may happen when I get older. I feel like if I get all the good stuff now, at a certain age something drastic could happen—like with my mom.

The most drastic thing would be to be paralyzed.

Just to be there, not talking, not moving, just alone with your thoughts. You can't tell no one what you want to eat or even do the things you used to do. Now I can play basketball and Genesis. I do it every day, 'cause I don't know if something drastic could happen to me.

I think all the bad things that happen are lessons. You learn something from every one that happens. Some lessons are more severe than others. I know you should enjoy all you have, while you have it.

If There Were No

Drugs Even if all the drugs would leave tomorrow, it would be hard, 'cause a lot of people are addicted. They would be saying that they need it, and there would be a desperate, desperate cry for drugs. Then, after a while, they would say, "I lived my life six months without drugs. Maybe I don't really need drugs. Hey, I have a life. Now, 'cause I don't spend money on drugs I can pay my bills." People would be more friendly waking up not worried about where they're going to get drugs. Without drugs, there would still be a struggle, but if people see that kind of life is possible, they may want to really live. It's like a job, using drugs. You're working twenty-four hours. You never have time off. You're always thinking about how or when you'll get them. If there were no drugs, people could just be living for twenty-four hours.

The Truth Hurts

It hurts when I hear people from outside where I live talk about the bad things in my neighborhood. Not 'cause the things aren't true. It hurts 'cause they know about it and aren't doing anything. They know all this stuff about it and criticize it, but that's that. They push it aside 'cause they don't want to do nothing about it.

It's a big problem. It's about money and expense. It costs too much money to change. Is money more important than the life of a child?

If you know what's bad in a place, you should think about learning and helping. It should come from the heart. If they are criticizing, it should be about change.

What I Learned About Love

My mom taught me how to love someone. She was always a loving person, no matter what. She always forgave the people she loved. Once someone in her family had robbed us, but she forgave them. She still loved him with all her heart. That's the way she loved my father and me.   **from Mom**

Parents with HIV

Many people I know have this new problem. Their parents are HIV-positive. I have one friend with both parents being HIV-positive. It doesn't really bother him 'cause he says they're not sick now. So a lot of the kids are not affected till they see their parents suffering and going through the stages.

Some people with HIV don't get sick right away and may not get sick for a while. But in a way it's bad, 'cause the kids don't think about it till it affects them. Then it just hits them. They worry but don't talk about it. A lot of people don't like to talk about their parents being sick.

I thought about it and think it's just a lesson. I'm not scared to say my parents are sick, 'cause a lot of people around my block know it already. I'm open to it. The best advice I have is to love your parents as much as you can, 'cause they could be okay one day and the next day you could lose them. Be prepared for it so later you don't say, "I should have done this. I should have done that."

One Less Victim

Sometimes I imagine I could fall victim to stuff. It's scary, 'cause I know I have to be on the lookout for myself and can never rest. The minute you rest and say, "I'm too powerful for that," you let your guard down. That's the biggest mistake in your life. Everyone could fall victim.

I've seen kids that I thought were strong fall victim to drugs. The other day, I was with two kids coming home from basketball practice. We saw some other kids we know. The next thing, the two kids I was with were sitting down smoking blunts with the others. My friends offered me, but I said no. The other kids said, "He won't. He wants to be a basketball player. Hasn't used it yet." It made me feel kind of good. They already know my status. I'm not with them. The kids that were with me then felt bad. One of them just stopped smoking and left. But they still did it.

Anyone can just start, even me. A lot of people get drunk. They think that's cool. To me, when I get older, I don't want to need drugs, alcohol, and cigarettes. Maybe then I'll take a beer after a basketball game, but it's tricky. There's a lot of people who drink or do drugs only on special occasions, but it's a way to start. You have to always watch yourself.

Overwhelmed

There's times that I think to myself, "If they haven't stopped all the bad things happening in my neighborhood, when are they going to stop it?" How bad do they want it to get? It's so bad now, I can't imagine how much worse it's going to be. What new disease or how much more drugs are going to kill people?

The cops, the government, and the FBI look at the drug dealers as small problems. They're looking at kilos of drugs and not what's going on at the street corners and all that. They're looking for big-time drug dealers from, like, Colombia.

So I worry. How bad does it have to get before they actually change it? I feel overwhelmed by it. It's confusing to the kids. Things are bad, and nothing's being done. You feel like nothing will ever be done.

A Change
for Hope

We need more things for youth to get into. A lot of places that do that sort of thing are scared to move to my neighborhood 'cause they hear about drug dealers, shootings, and everything. They don't try to build a YMCA or Boy's Club 'cause they are kind of nervous about that. If they would do it, it would be good, 'cause the kids would have a place to relax and play some ball.

They used to leave the schools open later, but they don't do it anymore. They do it in some places, but after a while kids don't go 'cause it's not close to their homes. It has to be schools in the kids' neighborhood. Kids won't make it their business to go out of their way, like to have to take a bus or train. It's too much time and then it costs, too.

The activities kids need have to go beyond sports, too. They need to learn about the problems that a lot of people go through. Like using drugs, thinking of suicide, or your parents being HIV-positive. You could have a youth program and talk about different subjects: AIDS, sex, drinking, and all that. Also, they should have new things to try, like computers, art, cultural stuff. This way, kids will see options instead of what's all around them.

Summer
of Togetherness

I'm just going to stay home with my father this summer and not go to summer school. Me and him are going to have this summer together. We're going to have fun with each other. That's all we're going to do. I think I'll be ready to start the tenth grade, anyway, 'cause I don't think the ninth grade was that hard and I caught up. I'll see. But this summer is for me and my dad.

Veronica:
Midway
to
Success

My dad told me I got a letter from Veronica. The letter said that she thought I had a lot of guts for going to her dad and that no other guy had ever done it. She invited me to go to her house for her birthday. I couldn't go, but I bought her a present.

I called her and finally spoke with her. I told her I bought her a present, and she was surprised. Me and dad had went to the stores to buy her the present. I bought her this dress that's in style. It's like a V-cut with some shorts. I would like to see her in it. That would be nice. I'm going to give it to her on Monday, 'cause she works near where I live.

I didn't think I would ever talk to her, but there I was. It was fun. She told me that her mom already thinks we're going out. It seems like now it's okay with her parents, but I don't know. I got to stick around a little more. She told me she's looking forward to coming to see me.

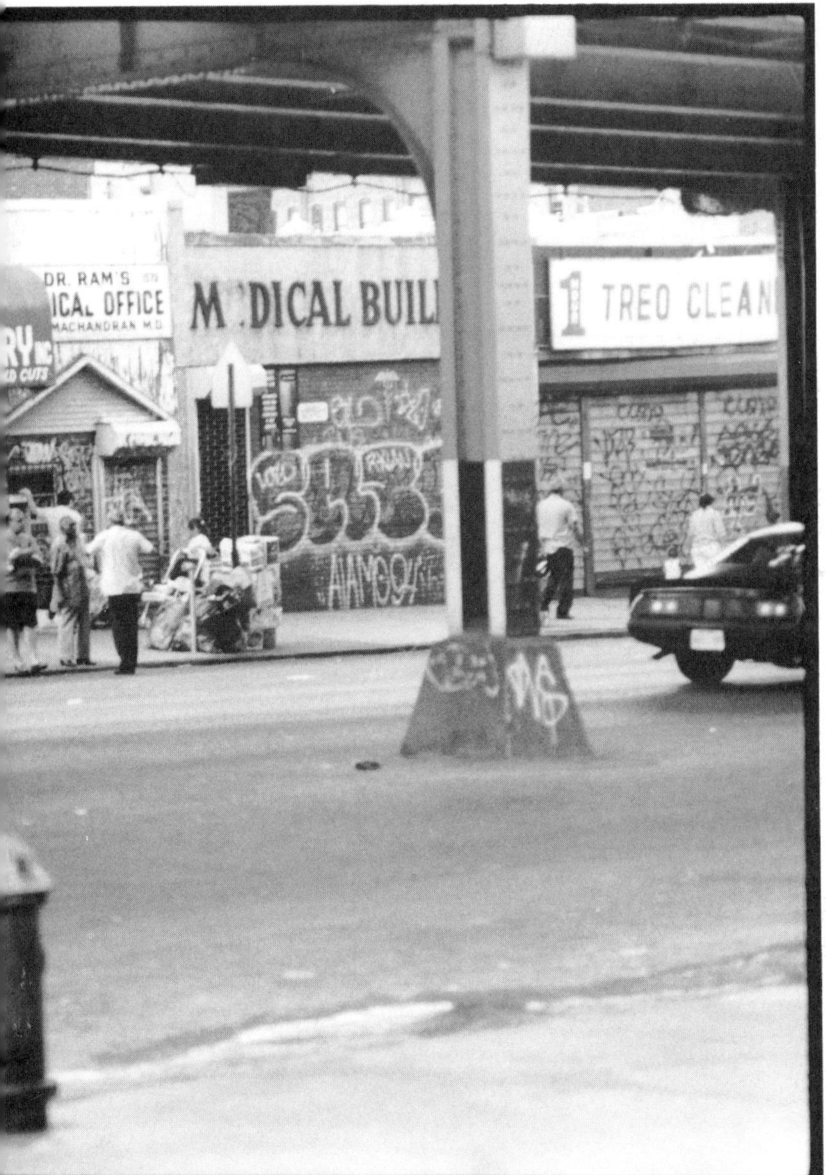
DR. RAM'S
ICAL OFFICE
MACHANDRAN M.D.
M DICAL BUIL
TREO CLEAN

A Good Parent

A good parent is strict about certain rules. Certain rules should be, like, changeable and certain rules should be strict. I mean like going outside. There should be a certain time you should go outside and a certain time you come back. It shouldn't be too early or too late. Some parents don't care if their kids stay out or even sleep out all night.

It's bad, 'cause kids have to know responsibility. How can kids learn to be strict on themselves if they never know rules? Getting up for school now will some day be getting up for work. A good parent gets the message across that we all have rules to live by.

The Big Problem in My Neighborhood

The real worst part of my neighborhood is the drug dealers. It's a horrible thing to see drug dealers and the kids involved with them. When I walk out of my house, I see all these drug dealers standing on the corner. They are next to the pay phone, the pizzeria, and all the stores. Everyone knows where it's happening.

It's bad, 'cause you see them selling to mothers and parents who should be taking care of their kids. If they're selling drugs to parents, these parents can't be taking care of their kids. They are on drugs and need their money for drugs. It upsets me 'cause it's right there and there's violence, people fighting.

I seen someone get shot. There was an argument. I don't know if it was a customer or just someone the guy knew. One guy is saying, "This is my block. If I tell someone not to sell you drugs, they're not going to sell you anything." They had a big argument. They were both big, and one guy was in the other's face. The other guy had his hands in his drawers and pulled out a gun and said, "What now, nigger?" The other guy said, "No, no! Hey, what's up? What are you doing?!" Then the first guy just pointed the gun at him and shot his foot. So this guy starts limping across the street yelling at the guy with the gun: "You punk ass nigger. I can't believe you shot me in the foot." Then he went into a store. The guy with the gun followed him and said, "What you mean 'punk-ass nigger'?" So the guy that got shot yells, "No, no! I can't believe you shot me in the foot!" Then the cops were coming 'cause of the gunshots, so the guy with the gun left 'cause he had to.

The cops never break up the corner, but there's, like, too many places anyway. The hottest area is Watson. The whole neighborhood, like three or four blocks, is all drugs. Drugs here, drugs there, drugs everywhere. There are even drugs in the stores. There are a lot of candy stores, but in the back they sell drugs. They just put up a store so the police won't think nothing of it. They put candy in this little small area, but the people don't go there to buy candy. The candy displays are there for the cops to see.

It would be hard to change this drug thing. It's too much. It's everywhere. It's too many people.

Relief

All my problems seem over. I still have problems, but not big problems. I know this 'cause I feel relief, I'm calm and comfortable. I feel good, like I could do anything I want. You know, free. I used to feel this way all the time, before everything happened to my mother, grandmother, and sister.

I learned that there are hard times to be had. I felt good at one moment and then, for a long while, I felt bad. It was like a nightmare that I couldn't wake up from. It happened so quickly, like a snap. But I see that if you just continue your life, it will get better.

If you think you're facing the hardest obstacle you have to face, just keep going. It's part of life. You're going to have your good times and bad times. It's just a matter of how well you'll get through the bad things. You have to go through it your own little way. You have to suffer it. But you will learn from the pain. You will understand what's going on in your life and know the kind of person you are.

Afterword

I think that a lot has happened since I started writing this book. And I learned a lot. There's good things and bad things but I'm gonna get through them like I have been getting through them. I want to show the best of myself and turn the worst things into the best things, the best things into better things.

My Dad showed me a lot and showed me how to get through situations and overcome the bad and to do what's best for me, how to look out for myself. I guess at this time his advice is helping me and that's why I love him for who he is deep inside. That's why you gotta look through the person to find their best quality 'cause everyone has a certain quality that should shine. Sometimes that quality is hard to find in someone, but if you reach inside, you find it. It just takes a little willpower, but it's there.

Photo Captions